AN EDUCATOR'S GUIDE TO
STEAM

AN EDUCATOR'S GUIDE TO
STEAM

ENGAGING STUDENTS USING REAL-WORLD PROBLEMS

Cassie F. Quigley
Danielle Herro

Foreword by Deborah Hanuscin

TEACHERS COLLEGE PRESS

TEACHERS COLLEGE | COLUMBIA UNIVERSITY

NEW YORK AND LONDON

Published by Teachers College Press, 1234 Amsterdam Avenue, New York, NY 10027

Cover design by Rebecca Lown. Cover photos by Betelgejze (background), Olena Yakobchuk (left inset), Paolo De Gasperis (center inset), Veja (right inset). All via Shutterstock.

Library of Congress Cataloging-in-Publication Data is available at loc.gov

ISBN 978-0-8077-6138-0 (paper)
ISBN 978-0-8077-6171-7 (hardcover)
ISBN 978-0-8077-7787-9 (ebook)

Printed on acid-free paper
Manufactured in the United States of America

26 25 24 23 22 21 20 19   8 7 6 5 4 3 2 1

Contents

Foreword

In my early education, I was a "good" student, which—back then—meant that I was well-behaved and pretty good at memorizing things. School was a place I went each day to learn things, but what I learned and my reasons for learning them had very little to do with my life outside of school. I could get an A on a science test, compete on the math team, or create original works for my AP art class—but I never considered how what I was learning about these subjects related to my community, how they were important to my role as a citizen in a democracy, or how it was relevant to my future career options. My learning was *disconnected*—not only were individual subjects taught in silos, but my world inside school was siloed off from the rest of the world. New approaches to teaching, such as STEAM education described in this volume, have recognized that in our increasingly complex world success is determined not by *what* you know, but by what you *can do* with what you know—such as the ability to critically evaluate evidence, make sense of information, and solve problems. To achieve this, learning must be *connected*—not only through the integration of disciplines, but through linkages that bring authenticity and relevance to students' engagement in learning activities.

When I became a teacher, I wanted the experiences of my students to be different from what I experienced as a learner. For example, during an ecosystem unit my 4th-grade class interacted with staff at our state Fish & Wildlife Conservation Commission, who helped them understand why specific species in our community were endangered. The students participated in habitat preservation projects in our outdoor classroom space to support biodiversity. They created a quilt featuring our state's endangered species, which later hung in our state capital, and composed public service announcements to air on our school's news channel. Throughout the unit, students developed and drew on skills in multiple disciplines as they extended their learning to the world beyond our classroom. Learning how to teach in this way required more than just a step-by-step guide or recipe to follow—I was imagining learning possibilities beyond my own experiences in school. In other words, I needed to have a *vision*. Herein lies the true value of the volume that you have picked up; not only will you understand what STEAM education is, you will also form a clear vision for STEAM education: What that could look like in your school or classroom and how to go about achieving that.

Cassie Quigley and Danielle Herro have compiled their years of experience working with teachers into a useful tool to guide individual teachers or entire schools in undertaking the ambitious transdisciplinary teaching of STEAM—science, technology, engineering, arts, and mathematics—in ways that promote students' engagement through *connected learning*. Their conceptual model for STEAM teaching comes to life in numerous classroom examples that illustrate problem-based approaches, curricular integration, and multiple pathways for creating lessons that are relevant to students and connected to their communities and interests. In addition to practical strategies, this book provides an excellent bridge between research and practice. As promised, readers will find it easier to plan for, design, and enact STEAM learning in K–8 schools and preservice teaching programs.

As a teacher, and now teacher educator, I understand the complexity of teaching and the difficulty of enacting change in one's practice—such as shifting to STEAM teaching. The authors of this book do due diligence in unpacking this complexity and discussing specific barriers teachers and schools might face in this undertaking. More importantly, they provide inspiration to sustain readers through this challenging work by emphasizing the rewards for both students and educators who engage in STEAM education.

—Deborah Hanuscin, PhD,
Western Washington University.

Acknowledgments

We wish to thank the countless administrators, teachers, and students who have opened their classrooms, communities, and hearts to us. We are particularly thankful for the many dedicated educators in Berkeley County Schools who partnered with us to create a strong vision for STEAM and in turn developed impressive STEAM units. Specifically, Gina Boyd, who has continued to support us and believe in our efforts while paving the way for many teachers and their students to excel in STEAM learning. We are fortunate to have worked closely with many excellent, hard-working educators and researchers who were willing to continually rethink and refine our collaborative work, and many students who gave us unbridled, honest feedback.

This book represents our collective efforts. We want to acknowledge Dr. Faiza Jamil, who helped us conceptualize initial drafts of the STEAM Conceptual Model. To Drs. George Petersen and Suzanne Rosenblith, we thank you for your leadership and vision, which helped to move our STEAM work forward in research and practice through the many doors that you opened for us. Your support for and trust in our efforts was always encouraging. We are grateful to our editor, Emily Spangler, for reaching out to us with this idea and supporting us through this process. We would also like to thank all our graduate students for their support and ideas, and especially Calli Shekell, who helped with the final edits. Finally, we are sincerely grateful to our families, and especially our husbands, Mark and Steve (AKA: the conference husbands) who have supported us as we traveled around the country working with educators, spent countless hours reviewing STEAM units, and had our heads buried deep in data or writing. This work is a labor of love for the field of education, to which we are deeply dedicated.

Introduction

Grounding Our STEAM Work

In 2012, the idea of STEAM (Science, Technology, Engineering, Art, and Mathematics) education started to gain momentum in innovative schools around the United States and several countries around the world. STEAM, where the "A" represents the arts and humanities, is an especially appealing way to increase participation in STEM fields through efforts that, according to the Educational Testing Service (2015), begin "in elementary school and extends through the professoriate and the rest of the workforce" (p. 3). Proponents of STEAM argue that integrating art is essential for innovation, as it provides an interesting, different, and collaborative way to view the world, adding that art prevents the disconnect of math and science from real-world applications (Wynn & Harris, 2012).

Interestingly, many communities and educators began embracing STEAM as a more creative and appealing way to engage students, though without sharing a common understanding of what it meant or how it should look in classrooms. STEAM programs in schools typically emphasized more art and technology offerings such as using robots to teach programming or coding, or they focused on integrated science curriculums with attention to engineering activities. Many of the programs were very good, but most were in after-school programs, summer camps, or specialized classes that attracted smaller numbers of students. Knowing that, historically, late-elementary and middle school girls and students of color often opt out or feel excluded from STEM-related coursework or opportunities has increased STEM programs aimed at underrepresented populations (Hill, Corbett, & St. Rose, 2010). Throughout this book we detail our desire to make STEAM appealing to all students. This is a direct response to addressing the lack of inclusion and diversity in STEM.

OUR ENTRY INTO STEAM EDUCATION

At the same time that STEAM was gaining popularity, a school district offered us an opportunity to conduct summer professional development with a motivated group of teachers at a school slated to open as a STEAM school the following fall. The administrators and teachers in the school believed that STEAM, whatever it looked like, should be offered to all their students—not just to those who could participate in after-school, summer programs, or elective courses. They wanted to have a common understanding of STEAM to guide the ways they might integrate it into their standard curriculum.

As former teachers with a great interest in science and technology education, we knew there had to be a better way to reach all kids, engage them in "school subjects," and get them excited to learn. We also knew from our earlier K–12 teaching days that kids often work hard to master skills or learn concepts if they care about the problem they are solving. We knew their engagement increased when the issues posed were interest-based, that is, when they were directly related to their families, communities, or lives.

As we talked on the phone one night, we discussed the work we were already doing with interest-based learning, technology enabled instruction, and project-based learning. We believed we could draw on ways these current approaches can lead to effective instruction, and we decided that they needed to be a significant part of whatever STEAM work we might do with teachers. We saw STEAM instruction as especially appropriate in K–8 classrooms, where teachers often seek ways to integrate content or disciplines. We also realized that our best ideas and efforts needed research to back them up. Thus, our work with teachers and simultaneous long-term research project began.

The goal of this book is to provide a common understanding of STEAM teaching and learning. For educators, we offer a blueprint for implementing STEAM instruction, and for educational researchers, we offer our evidenced-based strategies to consider when examining the efficacy of STEAM learning. Thus, this book is a natural next step in our progression to provide broad support, and a "how-to" of sorts for teachers, teacher educators, administrators, instructional coaches, and researchers who want to embark on providing STEAM instruction or develop a deeper understanding of it. We hope that by reading this book and using the STEAM conceptual model and numerous suggestions and examples throughout, STEAM educators will find it easier to plan, design, and enact STEAM learning in K–8 schools and preservice teaching programs. Additionally, while the stories, schools, students, and teachers are real, the names of teachers, students, and schools are pseudonyms throughout the book in order to protect their identities.

AN EXAMPLE OF STEAM IN ACTION

Mr. Samson stood in front of his 6th-grade classroom at Hunter Middle School showing a short video of a robotic pack mule moving up a mountainside that demonstrated the functions and modes of robotic devices.

Students had just finished brainstorming the economic impact of using robots to complete work on a Google Doc. After the video, he posed questions to his students about the pack mule's power source. One student, Eli, incorrectly answered that it was "battery-powered" before his classmate Jillian quickly explained that it was too high-powered for batteries, so it had to be a gasoline engine. Mr. Samson nodded his head in affirmation while projecting the STEAM scenario used to guide students' problem solving on the Promethean Board in the front of the room. It read:

> In 2016, *The Wall Street Journal* ran a story about robot-powered lawn mowers that resemble a Roomba® and travel around people's yards to keep them neatly trimmed. These mowers run on batteries, are fairly quiet, and can be scheduled to operate whenever a homeowner chooses. A number of companies have shown great interest in marketing them, seeing them as innovative, efficient, good for the environment, and profitable. However, there are still some issues with these robotic lawn devices in that they require a lot of time to set up and must be easily programmable to allow for sharp angles on small yards, and they must be able to stop and change directions if they hit something such as children's toys, hoses, trees, or lawn ornaments. Your project team has been hired to design, create, and present a marketing plan for an easy-to-use, effective robot mower. After creating a prototype and social media marketing plan, you will pitch your idea, *Shark Tank*–style, to a panel of experts.

This was the third STEAM scenario that Mr. Samson created this year after completing a week of summer professional development (PD) aimed at helping teachers conceptualize and implement STEAM instructional practices. Teachers used scenarios to introduce each unit and to engage students in relevant problem solving and mimic what might happen in the real world. The hope was students would begin to make connections to future STEM-related skills and jobs they might encounter with similar problems. STEM (Science, Technology, Engineering, and Math) is recognized as a way to bridge the discrete disciplines of science, technology, engineering, and mathematics using applications or processes from each to create knowledge as a whole (Morrison, 2006). However, STEM does not specifically attend to the arts and humanities, and it has been criticized for favoring particular subject areas (i.e., math and science, or engineering and technology).

Being able to solve real-world problems continues to be a goal of STEM education—and at times, education in general (Bybee, 2010). However, despite efforts to increase interest in STEM education and jobs, our nation continues to experience a shortage in STEM workers in that we are "not producing enough STEM-capable students to keep up with demand both in traditional STEM occupations and other sectors across the economy that demand similar competencies" (Carnevale, Smith, & Melton, 2011, p. 10). In fact, while the STEM graduation rates increased (Jaschick, 2014), students are not choosing to pursue STEM-related jobs (Masata, 2014).

One reason for this continued shortage is that students often believe this narrow approach to STEM allows little room for fields involving the arts and humanities. STEM graduates, despite their interest in science, technology, engineering, and math, want to pursue fields that incorporate creativity and the arts (U.S. Census Report, 2010). Therefore, educational leaders called for more balanced approaches to teaching and learning, which includes the arts, design, and humanities (Brady, 2014; Connor, Karmokar, & Whittington, 2015).

The trend toward offering STEAM instruction in classrooms or adopting STEAM as a curricular approach for entire schools is increasing. STEAM teaching has been noted in K-12 across the United States, in Europe, and throughout much of Korea (Delaney, 2014). A few early adopters of the approach in the United States include Andover High School in Massachusetts, Da Vinci Schools in California, Drew Charter School in Georgia, Fisher STEAM Middle School in South Carolina, Quatama Elementary School in Oregon, and Pulaski Middle School in Virginia. However, one difficulty in implementing STEAM teaching is the lack of agreement about what constitutes STEAM. Williams (2013) notes that some believe strong K–12 STEAM programs include creative or innovative math, science, or engineering teaching methods in which students are given presentation options. STEAM learning is aligned with robotics challenges, computer programming, media arts inclusion, or "Grand Challenges" (http://www.engineeringchallenges. org), which are endorsed by the National Academy of Engineering. Grand Challenges initially focused on postsecondary student engineers, challenging them to solve some of the world's most pressing problems. In recent years they have trickled into after-school programs primarily aimed at teens. In a 2014 *Education Week* article, Anne Jolly points out that STEAM should include attention to the arts in an applied manner, just like science or math. She first suggests that little consensus exists toward features of a quality STEM program in K-12, and then cites the American Society for Engineering Education's identification of excellence, which includes motivating contexts, application of math and science content, student-centered teaching methods, engineering challenges, teamwork, and communication with a focus on critical and creative thinking.

Jolly says, "STEM, then, is a specific program designed for a specific purpose—to integrate and apply knowledge of math and science in order to create technologies and solutions for real-world problems, using an engineering design approach. It's no surprise that STEM programs need to maintain an intense focus" (p. 18).

She discusses the appeal of STEAM, proposing that STEM projects can serve as a gateway to STEAM for underserved students when the elements of design, performing arts, or creative planning are included; she also cautions that art not be an add-on but instead approached naturally through the problem.

Attending to STEAM learning by including multiple disciplines, integrating technology, or challenging students with relevant problems is undeniably important. However, the fact remains that conversations similar to the one above have focused more on ideas and predictive reports, and included little empirical data from K–12 classrooms to guide researchers and educators (Quigley & Herro, 2016). This growing national and global attention to STEAM creates a need to support effective STEAM teaching and implementation practices.

THE PURPOSE AND USEFULNESS OF THIS BOOK

The purpose of this book is to provide support for teachers, teacher educators, administrators, instructional coaches, and researchers who, like Mr. Samson, are attempting to engage students in classrooms through STEAM education practices.

A STEAM Conceptual Model

We propose a conceptual model and then use connected learning theory to expand the model to suggest why and how teachers might approach implementing STEAM instructional practices. The STEAM conceptual model focuses on the classroom environment that teachers create, the ways in which they integrate the content, and the skills teachers will support during their teaching. The model includes specific strategies for teachers to implement, such as problem-based learning, incorporation of student choice, technology integration, and teacher facilitation.

Connected Learning

Connected learning draws on students' interests and equitable participation to support academically oriented, peer-networked, purposeful learning to solve relevant STEAM problems. Connected learning considers students' interests and uses technology to connect youth with their community, mentors, schools, and homes to practice real-world skills. In our research and in this book, connected learning guides STEAM instruction in two primary ways: (1) as a means to draw on students' interest in choosing relevant, real-world problems to solve when designing STEAM problem-solving scenarios (e.g., local issues they care about and can relate to that have a STEAM focus), and (2) to provide engaging ways to demonstrate learning based on what students participate readily in outside of school, such as video production, digital drawing/sketching, and visual and collaboration tools, when developing and sharing creative solutions to problems.

As we step back into the classroom, we see Mr. Samson working with his students during their fifth day of the STEAM unit. Students are busy working in groups of three to program their robot using a Lego Mindstorms kit (https://www.lego.com/en-us/mindstorms), following a design they had sketched in SketchUp (https://www.sketchup.com), an online 3D modeling program. Walking from group to group, our research team interacted with the students, talking to them about the problem, asking them to show us what step they were on and to explain retests and revisions they were making in their code. One student tested his gyro sensor, a device that senses and measures angles, and realized it turned too wide, so he asked members of the group to help him adjust the program. Another group was collaboratively trying to solve ways to fix the program because the robot stopped after two turns, and a third group was busy watching a video of a Google Hangout session recorded the previous day with a panel of local community members who worked as engineers. Mr. Samson spent the majority of the class period checking in with each group, providing advice and at times taking students to the side of the room to work with them. He reminded them that they would be presenting solutions to their challenges to a "company" interested in buying their product, and he let them choose digital media and tools for their presentation.

Aligning the conceptual model described above with Mr. Samson's classroom demonstrates how his classroom environment fostered problem-based learning, which was delivered through a relevant scenario drawing on a real-world problem that was detailed in a news article. The various disciplines emerged naturally through the problem as students used science to understand principles of energy, math to calculate angles, and program software to engineer a design. The humanities were addressed both through the media arts as well as discussing the economic and social issues related to innovation and the workforce. Technology served as the backbone for much of the collaborative work, including digital design, prototyping, and marketing. Students were given the opportunity to choose groups, technologies, and problem-solving strategies, and they were encouraged to ask new questions. Mr. Samson facilitated the learning through technology and circulating in the classroom versus direct instruction. When considering connected learning, this STEAM unit drew on students' interests in current events, robotics, technology, and social media marketing. The unit was designed to allow them to participate equitably when working in groups, acknowledging their various skills (e.g., some excelled at programming and math, others at media arts, and still others at presentation skills). Their teacher, peers, community members, and experts supported students as they practiced real-world skills.

Mr. Samson was involved in our early work in STEAM education, and teachers like him were the reason we became interested in further exploring the potential of STEAM as an instructional approach. We came into this work because a nearby large school district where Mr. Samson taught was opening a state-of-the-art STEAM school with great enthusiasm, remarkable spaces for collaboration and interaction, and an ambitious vision, but the school district had a limited conceptualization of what STEAM instruction might look like. As we began to research STEAM, we quickly realized that numerous schools have emerged supporting the inclusion of the "A" in STEM, promoting both the arts and humanities to assist in STEM learning (Delaney, 2014), yet there is little research on STEAM teaching practices in K–12 classrooms (Kim & Park, 2012). There are schools across the country and world that are shifting their focus to include STEAM instruction without a solid understanding of how to support teachers in this transformation.

Research and STEAM Teaching Guiding This Book

As we began to work with this new STEAM school and other schools, we saw an opportunity to engage students through this type of instruction and wanted to provide guidance to teachers. This book is the culmination of 5 years of longitudinal research on STEAM professional development and classroom implementations of STEAM teaching, working with more than 150 teachers through numerous summer professional development experiences and in classrooms in three large school districts in the Southeastern United States. We analyzed hundreds of teachers' reflective journal entries and STEAM unit plans, interviews, observations of teachers' instruction in their classroom, and teacher and student artifacts.

From this work, we found that effective STEAM teaching involved positioning teachers to create problem-solving scenarios foregrounding problems for students to solve, using creative and collaborative skills that encompass various disciplines. This is distinctly different from typical STEM instructional approaches, which often begin with the discipline or content and have students solve explicit problems that often stop short of connecting their problem solving to real-world, social or humanitarian issues (Herro & Quigley, 2016).

STEAM Teaching Versus Content-Focused Teaching

STEAM is also best taught in a transdisciplinary manner. Transdisciplinary teaching means that the problem is foregrounded during problem solving and the disciplines emerge naturally through it. Transdisciplinary teaching takes skill and practice, so we devote Chapter 4 to understanding ways to effectively apply it to STEAM teaching. While STEAM certainly aims to teach content, it is problem-focused as opposed to content- or discipline-directed.

To illustrate the difference between the two approaches, we provide examples below:

STEAM teaching:

> Just 8 days ago there was an earthquake of a 2.0 magnitude in Cityview! In fact, earthquakes happen all the time and are becoming more and more prevalent. While most are minor, and we cannot even feel the earth shifting, significant earthquakes cause severe damage and have the potential to harm and kill people. Your task is to determine whether or not a significant earthquake could ever take place in Cityview. Your team will gather evidence to support and defend your answer. To communicate this information to the public, you must create an informational brochure or video expressing your claim.

Content-focused teaching:

> The objectives of the unit, although not stated in the example, are to infer an earthquake's epicenter from seismographic data, explain how earthquakes result from forces inside Earth, and identify and illustrate geologic features of Cityview and other regions of the world. During the unit, the class will use topographic maps to analyze data. From these data, students will draw a map of the state marking the epicenters and fault lines.

To further highlight the differences between the approaches, consider that STEAM teaching includes:

1. *Problem solving* through a real-world application in which there is no definite answer (e.g., the students are asked to determine whether or not a major earthquake could ever take place in their state, predict the epicenter, and discuss the potential impact).
2. *Multiple disciplines* are acknowledged in the scenario, which incorporates the use of several disciplines. The example above may include engineering practices to determine the impact of the earthquake on the state's infrastructure, English language arts to communicate evidence, science concepts explored during the investigations on earthquakes and epicenters, technology integrated by using visualization tools (e.g., infographics) or videos (e.g., Adobe Spark or iMovie), and social studies integrated through exploring geography of epicenters and landforms or the political decisionmaking processes. Engineering design practices may also

be employed during the assessment of the current infrastructure, and the creative arts might be incorporated if students create music that evokes the feelings of a natural disaster or write a poem about emotions that arise during an earthquake.

3. *Collaborative skills* are required to present a solution as students are placed in teams to solve the problem. Creative skills can be employed throughout the project but are notably seen in the use of visualization tools, as well as the emotional impact of the problem.

We argue that STEAM education is a more powerful teaching and learning approach, as it encourages students to encounter new questions or lines of inquiry. For instance, in the earthquake example, they might become curious about why earthquakes are increasing in number and magnitude or consider precautions that should be taken, current safety measures, and how city councils operate and interact with the public. On the other hand, the discipline-focused approach relies on science standards to have students explore the problem where all the students use the same tools, with a goal of producing the same answer.

In addition, during our research we found that this type of STEAM instructional approach is more equitable. As professors of science education and digital media and learning at large public universities serving rural, suburban, and urban areas, we are keenly focused on underserved populations and equity in learning experiences. Cassie is a former middle and high school science teacher with nearly a decade of experience in classrooms. Her current research is focused on increasing student engagement in science, and she sees STEAM as a way to connect students to science in their everyday lives through problem-solving approaches. Dani, a former elementary teacher, computer resource teacher, and instructional technology administrator, uses her experiences with enacting and scaling up interest-based, technology-rich, and content-focused problem solving to STEAM education. We recognize that these ideas can be implemented with greater ease in after-school and gifted and talented programs and charter or other settings; however, that is not the goal of this book. We are committed to public education, and chose to conduct this research in those settings. The teachers in this book represent public school teachers who are bound by the realities of accountability and standardized testing. The teachers implemented these practices during the academic year, and during their regular instructional time. We suggest that these opportunities are for all students, not only for those who are able to attend camps or after-school clubs. For us, it only makes sense to do this work to impact the more than 50 million students in public schools throughout the United States.

STEAM instruction, as conceptualized in our work, reflects the work of dedicated teachers who aim to serve and engage all students. We believe that in order to affect real change in classrooms and impact learning, we first need to focus on effective instruction and shifting practice, recognizing the realities of standards-based, content-focused classrooms while building bridges with teachers to connect expertise, community issues, and student-centered learning. Therefore, this book captures ways in which teachers learn about and enact STEAM instruction in their classrooms based on the use of a conceptual model introduced in Chapter 1 to guide STEAM unit planning.

THE ORGANIZATION OF THE BOOK

An Educator's Guide to STEAM is organized in three sections to provide the context for STEAM education and include ways to conceptualize STEAM and develop STEAM units for classrooms that make STEAM education successful across contexts—whether your school allows for single-classroom STEAM instruction or collaborative or team teaching of STEAM units, or is dedicated to fully adopting STEAM teaching as part of its mission.

To that end, Part I assists in conceptualizing STEAM by providing a useful model to set the stage to vision, plan, and support STEAM learning. We then expand this model using connected learning theory to guide more equitable STEAM instruction when creating STEAM classrooms. We explore ways to make STEAM relevant to students by presenting and solving local community issues and attending to humanistic (e.g., arts and humanities) approaches to engage students. Part II begins with an in-depth discussion of transdisciplinary teaching and includes a chapter on arts integration. Part III provides guidance for how to assess STEAM learning and offers ways to make STEAM work in a variety of contexts, including traditional and STEAM-focused schools. We also discuss the challenges of STEAM education in order to consider ways to alleviate them. Finally, in the conclusion, we take a look at the future of STEAM education.

Part I

CONCEPTUALIZING STEAM

CHAPTER 1

Unpacking the Conceptual Model to Guide STEAM Teaching

In this chapter, we will examine what STEAM is and how teachers implement the practices in their classrooms. We provide examples of each of the instructional strategies that compose the STEAM conceptual model and align this model to the theoretical framework that undergirds it, connected learning theory. To do this, we begin by looking at a 6th-grade classroom where Ms. Brown was the science teacher. As a part of the science curriculum, students studied the life cycle of organisms and habitats. Ms. Brown felt this standard was an opportunity to utilize STEAM education to engage her students in solving a real-world problem that was happening at the local zoo. She researched the problem and contacted the local zoo to find out more information about it and to inquire if they would be interested in partnering with her 6th-graders in solving their problem. She was pleased when the zoo was very willing to partner with the school. Being able to draw on real-world problems and ones that are locally relevant is one component of STEAM teaching. The problem she developed through her research and conversations with the zoo was:

> Sadly, the elephants, Lady Bird and Joy, have died. As a result, there is a large space open. The zoo wants to fill the space with a new animal but doesn't know which animal to choose. The zookeepers are inviting middle schools to weigh in on the decision. The 6th grade at Glenview Middle School will help to select the animal. As a part of this project, you will research what animal should move into this space. To do so, you need to examine what the recommendations are for the animals' living space, and understand the animals' living habits and life cycles. After coming up with the list of possible animals, you will survey the entire school to see which animal should live in the enclosure, and then create an interactive presentation to convince the zookeepers of this choice.

Ms. Brown placed this problem on the SMART Board. The students sat at tables facing one another with their school-issued laptops open. The atmosphere was light, with the sounds of students clicking on their computers and the low rumble of them talking to one another. Ms. Brown moved from group to group, checking in on their initial ideas about the problem. Ensuring that students are able to direct some of the learning is another component of STEAM education. The reason is that it is one way the students become interested in the problem they are solving. Ms. Brown frequently made supportive comments encouraging the students to delve deeper into their research such as, "Interesting, I wonder if other zoos have similar problems?" A central aspect of STEAM teaching is this notion of teacher facilitation. A variety of instructional tools such as a problem-based approach to education help direct teacher facilitation in classrooms.

When I caught up with Ms. Brown between conversations with students, she was quick to describe the high level of engagement her students have when they work with STEAM problems. She stated:

> For them [the students], this is what they normally do, they use technology, talk to other people about it, form ideas, and create. And so, I don't have to convince them of this method. For me, this was a shift in my teaching. Yes, I used hands-on activities, but this is different. STEAM teaching uses a variety of strategies, so students are using different disciplines while solving problems.

STEAM: UNDERSTANDING THE RISING TREND

Increasingly, schools continue to adopt these types of STEAM practices for students (Henriksen, 2014). In fact, the New Media Consortium Horizon Report (Johnson, Adams-Becker, Estrada, & Freeman, 2015) listed STEAM as one of the rising trends in K-12 education, and STEAM-focused schools continue to appear in a variety of locales in the United States and around the world. However, most educators know little about STEAM teaching practices and how to address STEAM teaching in their classrooms. This problem is likely because educators struggle with a clear conceptualization of STEAM and how the disciplines (science, technology, engineering, arts and humanities, and math) might be connected (Guyotte, Sochacka, Costantino, Walther, & Kellam, 2015; Quigley & Herro, 2016).

Some argue that STEAM teaching, particularly in K–12, has been represented in strong STEM programs over the years through creativity and innovation in teaching methods and presentation options (Williams, 2013). These educators suggest that STEAM learning is demonstrated, for example, in engineering challenges that might be solved and shown in student-created videos, or offering students elective courses in computer programming or coding. The challenge is that these programs are often only offered after-school, or to a select group of students, instead of infusing them in the traditional school day. Others have interpreted the acronym STEAM to meet their curricular goals, proposing that "A" might address architecture or even agriculture. In general, these conversations have resulted in predictive reports or articles detailing classroom examples focused on sharing ideas. While necessary, the descriptions and plans are not comprehensive enough to offer teachers a model for implementing STEAM education in their classrooms. Instead, what often happens is that teachers utilize existing STEM curriculum and call it STEAM by adding a component of art (e.g., drawing, coloring, designing). The results of this type of implementation are mixed: Students either see this as so similar to their science and math classrooms that it does not engage them, or they do not see how the arts can be used beyond the visual arts.

The integration of STEM into other disciplines is immensely important. Interdisciplinary approaches can actually increase conceptual understanding of disciplines, while simultaneously increasing student interest (Harwell, Guzey, & Moore, 2016). Students demonstrate greater motivation and involvement, as well as learn more deeply, when they can apply classroom-gathered knowledge to authentic problems, and also when they take part in problem solving that requires sustained engagement and collaborative activities (Barron & Darling-Hammond, 2008).

For these reasons, our approach provides a transdisciplinary conceptual model that can be used in K–8 classrooms. With the increased adoption of STEAM education, there is an urgent need to provide a reliable approach to facilitate STEAM learning during classroom instruction that positively impacts students. In this chapter, we describe a conceptual model that offers specific strategies for teachers to create STEAM curricula mimicking skills found in STEM-related careers. The model supports teachers in designing problem-based curricula. The problems are rooted in scenarios aligned with real-world issues, drawing on students' interest in digital technology activities such as games, media, and video development as part of the problem-solving process. Thus, students are more likely to become aware of, and connected to, future STEM-related careers. Offering opportunities during the school day to all students is one way to broaden participation. Another opportunity for increasing participation is through relevant problem solving.

The goal of STEAM is to increase participation in school to ensure that *all* students are engaged. We view STEAM as a way to improve the involvement of all students in the areas of science, technology, engineering, arts, and mathematics. Often, when STEM is taught with a focus on content and standards, it disengages students. Additionally, because of the lack of women and people of color in the fields of science, math, engineering, and technology, students frequently point to the lack of mentors as the reason they do not go into or stay in STEM fields. In this way, STEM careers misrepresent the more significant population, including a gender gap and unequal representation of race and socioeconomic status (Gayles, 2011). Early findings on STEAM teaching practice demonstrate more participation from females and students of color (Sousa & Pilecki, 2013). For us, it is critical that this conceptual model incorporates ways in which teachers can support increased participation. Participation is increased by engaging students through a variety of strategies outlined in our conceptual model. We designed these procedures with the ideas that there are not low-level students and high-level students, but rather students who have developed the skills for certain tasks and students who are still developing those skills. Therefore, we view students as having multiple abilities. Creating instructional strategies from the standpoint of various abilities includes providing different ways of presenting the information, which will draw on multiple skills to be called upon to access or complete the activity.

Multiple-ability tasks are a way to shift what counts as "being smart" (Cohen, Lotan, Scarloss, & Arellano, 1999). Students who do not excel at traditional school tasks (i.e., multiple-choice tests) often shine when the content is presented in different ways, such as problem-based and inquiry-focused. In STEAM, the tasks the students complete require multiple abilities. In Ms. Brown's classroom, students created a variety of types of infomercials, including video-based, print, and interactive ones involving questionnaires and QR codes (the black-and-white codes that smartphone cameras are able to scan, which link to more information about the product). Remarkably, the teacher noted that students who were not previously interested in demonstrating their knowledge were the ones most engaged. Ms. Brown summed up this engagement through multi-ability tasks when she reflected:

> I realized how limiting traditional assessments could be. Yes, I can cross off whether the students know the content, or rather, they don't know the material. But after watching the students work together, each of them had their roles. Some were videoing and editing; others were writing scripts; other students researched the content and how to describe the information to an audience. And for the students who would normally not participate, they were the stars! One child, Maggie, really did great. She knew all this stuff about video editing. She ended up helping a bunch of the other groups too. And as a result of working with all the videos, she really understood about animals' habitats and life cycles.

As the teachers acknowledge the successes in multiple ways, other students begin to view the student who contributes in new ways positively (Pescarmona, 2014). Ms. Brown described how Maggie's status of being a low performer shifted: "The kids in the class would ask her all sorts of questions. She was the expert." It is important to note that Ms. Brown's school and classroom reflect the diversity in the local area, as the school is 52% White, 32% African American, 9% Latino, 2% multiple races, 2% Asian, and less than 1% American Indian or Pacific Islander, comparable to the United States. The school is 42% female and 58% male. In Ms. Brown's classroom, students are assigned groups to encourage the middle schoolers to work with different students, and so her tables are often mixed regarding race and gender. She often uses random groups as a strategy to encourage students to work with students they may not know well. She recognizes that this causes problems, but she remarked, "After a few weeks, this becomes normal. They work a lot together, but everyone has a different job, and so it is less group work and more doing the work and bringing the work together and blending the ideas."

EXPLORING THE STEAM CONCEPTUAL MODEL

Just as Ms. Brown noted above, "STEAM teaching uses a variety of strategies," and there are several interrelated strategies to STEAM teaching. These approaches make up the STEAM conceptual model and are helpful for guiding teachers as they integrate STEAM into their classrooms. In this model, we focus on the learning context, or the context the teachers create to facilitate STEAM learning. This includes how the teachers structure their classroom for STEAM and the ways they can integrate the disciplines based on this environment. It is critical to rethink the learning context so the school starts to mimic the ways people solve problems in the real world, which fosters students' problem-solving skills. Figure 1.1 is the STEAM conceptual model that includes the learning context of problem-solving skills, discipline integration, and the classroom environment. There are also two overarching components that thread through these components: authentic assessment and equitable participation.

Understanding the Overlap Between STEAM and Connected Learning

Part of this restructuring of the teaching process is to look at educational theories that can guide STEAM. One such theory is called connected learning (Ito et al., 2013). This theory "represents a framework for understanding and supporting learning, as well as a theory of intervention that grows out of our analysis of today's changing social, economic, technological, and cultural context" (p. 7). At the core of connected learning is an equity agenda examining the ways youth learn, given their wider access to "information, technology, and interest-driven communities" (Ahn et al., 2014, p. 2).

Connected learning looks to uncover and build collective capacity, identities, and opportunities. It acknowledges the variety of pathways that students bring to a learning experience and suggests that these pathways are often connected. Presently, much of the focus of connected learning has been on informal learning programs and online communities (Ahn et al., 2014). In our work we have found that connected learning aligns with STEAM

Figure 1.1. STEAM Conceptual Model

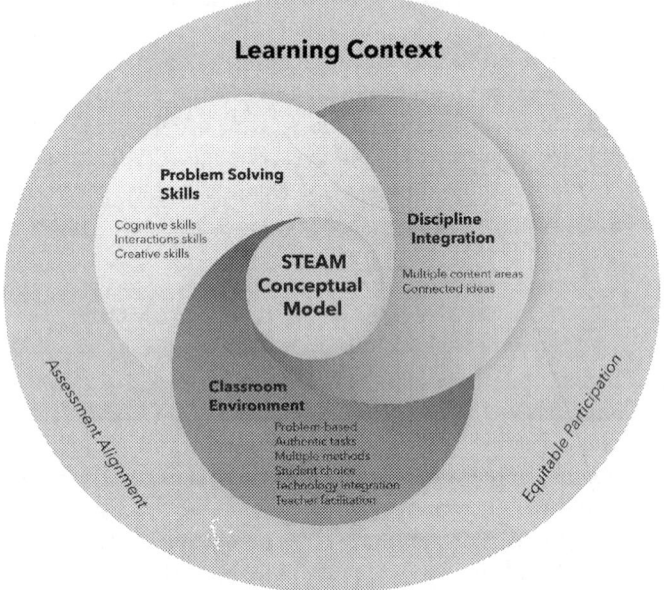

(Adapted from Quigley, Herro, and Jamil, 2017.)

education in two primary ways: (1) as a means to draw on students' interests to help teachers chose authentic, real-world problems to solve when designing STEAM problem-solving scenarios (e.g., local issues students have an interest in), and (2) tapping into the ways students learn outside of school, such as video production, digital drawing/sketching, and visual and collaboration tools (Grimes & Fields, 2012) when developing and sharing creative solutions to problems.

There is a growing body of research examining how learning is connected across settings and the relationship between in- and out-of-school learning. The premise of connected learning, which originated in the 1990s as Internet-related technologies became increasingly mainstream, is that to understand learning, one must understand the social processes situated in and across contexts. It draws on sociocultural and situated learning theory (Lave, 1988), emphasizing social learning situations and processes in everyday life.

In the last decade, researchers and educators have proposed connected learning theory as a way to conceptualize the impact of youth media production and expression across digital media networks, in particular when participants are creating or solving problems they care about. Figure 1.2 shows the connected learning framework (Ito et al., 2013) and the relationship between the principles:

Figure 1.2. Connected Learning Framework

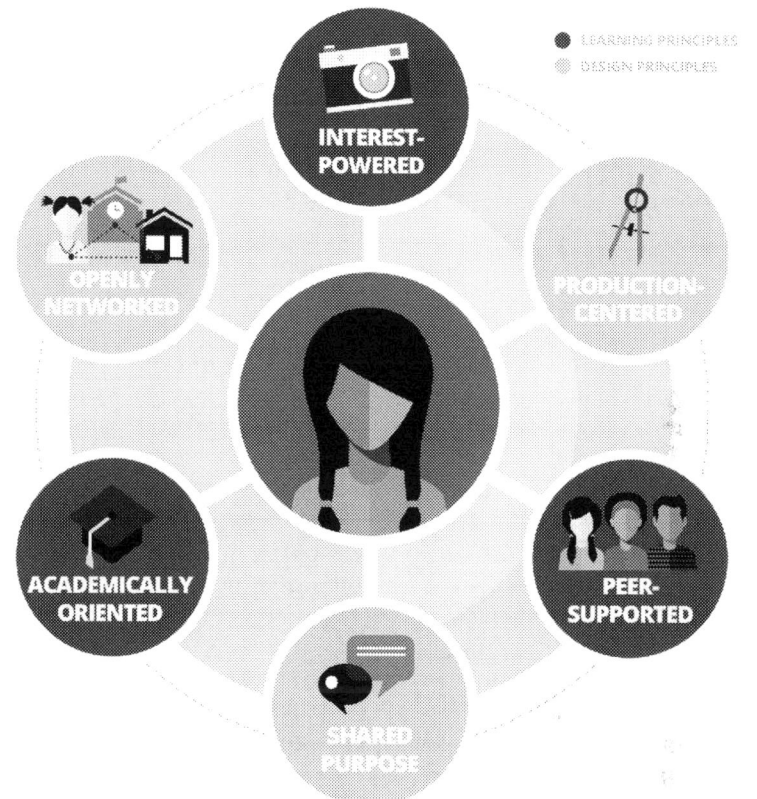

(Reprinted with permission from Ito et al., 2013.)

- *Learning Principles* (peer-supported, interest-powered, and academically oriented) make up the context for learning and can extend learning across home, community, and school settings.
- *Design Principles* (production-centered, shared purpose, openly networked) inform the intentional connections between active learning and how people participate.
- In this framework, technology is seen as the catalyst that provides opportunities for students as it fosters engagement and self-expression, increases accessibility, and expands social supports and diversity during interest-based learning.

The overlap between these principles intentionally provides multiple access and entry points for students who are often disconnected from traditional school settings. Connected learning experiences often result in these deeper learning experiences, which include systems thinking, creativity, persistence, and self-reflection.

Educational researchers and schools are particularly interested in connected learning for its potential to motivate learners and offer deep learning as children pursue personal interests with the support of peers and adults who recognize their skills and accomplishments (e.g., youth who create personal blogs detailing their everyday experiences in neighborhoods losing green space and play space due to urban sprawl, or videos created and shared via social media revealing the aftermath of a hurricane and asking for donations for family members or the local community). While connected learning is not common to formal schooling a small, but growing, number of innovative teachers are invested in the approach, believing that students learn best when they are allowed to create and solve problems they care about (What Is Connected Learning?, n.d.).

When we first became engaged in STEAM work, we saw this novel pedagogical technique as an opportunity to reengage with students through relevancy and creative problem solving. However, for schools to be able to implement connected learning theory, educators need a platform that can be aligned to the requirements of formal education. STEAM education offers ways to support teachers using connected learning as a guidepost to STEAM instruction. By tapping into connected learning, teachers can take how students learn best and infuse these skills into their classrooms. However, this requires teachers to think differently about how they structure their classrooms.

In our research, we found that there are several ways to support rethinking the ways teachers structure their classrooms. Specifically, when they include problem-based approaches, authentic tasks, multiple ways to solve the problem, student choice, technology integration, and teacher facilitation, this creates an environment supporting STEAM. Next, we describe what this looks like in Ms. Brown's classroom. At the end of this chapter, we will discuss ways this might look different at other grade levels.

Situating the STEAM Model in a Classroom

"So, I see you've decided on a koala for the empty enclosure. Can you tell me why?" Ms. Brown asked a group of four students, two girls and two boys. One of the girls, Starr, piped up, "Yes. We looked up the new size requirements, and now you have to have a lot more space for animals. It is the law." She pulled up her Google Doc as she was talking. "Here, it is." She pointed to the data table from the Central Zoo Authority. Ms. Brown nodded and said, "Okay, so let's go back to the problem the zoo gave us. What other considerations do you need to look at besides size?" Danny, one of the boys, responded, "We are worried about the amount of food they eat. They eat A LOT." Ms. Brown stated, "Good, so you are looking into that now?" Starr nodded. "Yeah, we are trying to figure out what other animals eat. But koalas don't eat meat, so they are cheaper to feed. Plus, they sleep a lot!"

Problem-Based Approach. When teachers situate the work in a real-world problem, such as the problem at the local zoo, it helps to make the problem and, by extension, the content more relevant to the students. This shift to introducing the material of the life cycles of animals with a problem changes the way teachers structure their classrooms. Ms. Brown discussed this: "Normally, I would have asked students to choose an animal to research, but it wouldn't have been a problem they were solving. Instead, they'd need to write about the life cycle and maybe do a presentation on the animal." To start with a problem, teachers create scenarios, such as the one about the zoo, that change the learning from the content to solving the problem. In addition, they are tapping into the interest-powered aspect of connected learning, and one that is academically oriented because of its alignment to the standards.

Authentic Tasks. Once the teachers write the scenario, they find the other strategies easier to implement. For example, in the zoo problem, the students went to the zoo to measure the enclosure and then compared that information with the space requirements for a variety of animals. This task is authentic because it helps to solve the problem and is something that would be done in the real world. This helps to provide an academically oriented space by creating opportunities for students to see the connection to civic engagement and careers. Conversely, tasks that are inauthentic or disconnected from the problem are often viewed as disjointed, and the students recognize them as schoolwork, often becoming disengaged. When the latter happens, teachers note that there is no alignment with the connected learning framework, as this would not be how students would actually solve the problem outside of school. At times in our research, we found that teachers sometimes shifted back to inauthentic tasks. Ms. Brown discussed this challenge: "During the zoo project, I used a lecture I created previously about different biomes [environments in the world], and I could see the students immediately disengage. I should have embedded it into the project instead." Although the content of the lecture was necessary, Ms. Brown recognized that engagement contributes to learning and that there are more authentic ways for students to learn about the different types of biomes.

Multiple Solutions. One of the goals of connected learning is providing an opportunity to engage students in learning. Intentionally connecting learning environments allows everyone to participate. When examining STEAM teaching practices, we found it critical to promote multiple methods to solve a problem, to not privilege one way of knowing or doing. Therefore, an instructional strategy supporting various methods or ways to address an issue is readily aligned with a learning environment that invites participation from students.

If the problem is indeed a real-world situation, there will be multiple ways to solve it. Another way for teachers to recognize if a problem allows for various solutions is to think about the final products the students will create and ask, "Will all the products look the same?" If so, then the problem only has one answer. If there will be a variety of products, then often there are a variety of solutions. In Ms. Brown's classroom students chose a variety of animals to fill the enclosure, including the sun bear, anteater, koala, and a butterfly garden. The way they persuaded the zookeepers was also based on a variety of reasons, including economics, exposure to new types of animals, and increasing the attendance to the zoo. When students are allowed to pursue different ways to solve a problem, this ensures that multiple abilities are necessary to solve the problem, which increases who participates and ways to demonstrate they are "smart."

Student Choice. Similarly, student choice helps to provide opportunities for students to express themselves in a variety of ways. To create a context for learning, connected learning can focus on these different ways of expression by creating interest-powered environments where learners can contribute expertise, ideas, and questions related to something that is personally satisfying to them. Student choice can most often be integrated into the final product, but also in the process. By allowing students to have options, they often have ownership over their learning, and engagement is high (Stefanou et al., 2004). We found that teachers feel more comfortable with incorporating student choice over time; they may initially start with one or two options for a final product, such as video or a blog. However, as Ms. Brown noted, "By the end of the year, the students were suggesting new ideas for the final product such as a video game or a skit, and as long as they met the requirements, I saw this as another way students could demonstrate success and mastery over the content."

Technology Integration. Technology integration is a critical component of STEAM and connected learning. The T in STEAM helps students engage in their world, which is increasingly more technological. However, our focus is on shifting from students as consumers of technology to producers of technology, because this is the way students primarily use technology outside of school. It is much different from what they are used to in schools. By shifting from consumers to producers, we change the focus from learning the technique of how to use technology to enhancing student learning *through* technology. Ms. Brown described this shift when she said, "Before I would focus on teaching the tool instead of using the tool to its full potential. I used to show YouTube videos; now my students MAKE the videos. It was hard at first because I worried I didn't know enough about how to do the technology. But the reality is, the students do. Or if we get stuck, we can work around the issues." Technology integration looks different across schools and depends significantly on access to resources. In Ms. Brown's classroom, the students each have their school-issued laptops. However, we acknowledge that this is not the case in all schools in the United States. That said, we noted that even in underresourced schools, during STEAM instruction, teachers were incredibly resourceful and used available digital tools and platforms to increase technology use for collaboration, production-oriented solutions, and presentations. At minimum, most schools sanctioned G Suite (formerly Google Apps for Education) and took students to a computer lab more frequently, had them share devices, or allowed older students to use their own devices. We noted STEAM classrooms regularly integrating digital tools such as Google Classroom, Docs, Forms, and Slides; video production; interactive graphs; infographics; and even video game creation.

Teacher Facilitation. As discussed in the first example, Ms. Brown was found working with small groups or individuals during STEAM learning. However, this does not mean that she never directs student learning. In our model, we focus on strategies that encourage more student-directed education, but there are moments when it looks very traditional. Teachers might be up in the front of the room asking questions about the ways to calculate population density and then guide much of the learning. Teacher-facilitated learning is often difficult for teachers. Ms. Brown discussed this transition. "At first, I didn't know how to redirect the students. The students came to me for the answers. We implemented '3 before me,' which means they are supposed to ask three people (or an online source) before coming to me. They have to tell me what they found first. This technique eliminated many questions and encouraged them to look to their peers as well." In our research, we noted that when teachers became more comfortable with the flexibility and fluidity of the process, so did the students. As Ms. Brown stated, "It is about being comfortable with not knowing what the exact answer is." Again, this mimics real-world problems, as they often do not have one correct answer. Instead, there are multiple solutions. Teacher facilitation in STEAM education aligns with multiple areas of connected learning, most notably that it is peer-supported. When teachers perceive the goal of STEAM education as being a way to create an environment where peers will work together, this shifts the learning to ways that are less teacher-directed.

Discipline Integration. Discipline integration is the way in which teachers connect multiple disciplines or content areas through a problem-based unit. While the model posits the goal of STEAM as transdisciplinary, the model also looks at the different levels of discipline integration (one content area or discipline, multiple disciplines, interdisciplinary, and transdisciplinary). Teachers are more readily able to integrate various disciplines when they align the disciplines to the problem to be solved. When the ideas are connected, there is an apparent integration of the subjects so that the knowledge from all disciplines contributes to solving the problem. In Ms. Brown's classroom, students were drawing on the content of math, science, ELA, art, and social studies. For example, some students looked at the history of zoos and learned how some countries opened zoos after significant events such as wars, or how a zoo in Warsaw, Poland, was a hiding place to save hundreds of Jews during World War II.

Teachers required all groups to use math skills to understand the dimensions of the space and whether or not the new animal would have enough area according to the regulations. The students also investigated habitats and life cycles of the animals. A group of three students was interested in having a sun bear (an Asian bear) and wondered, "Do they hibernate like other bears? Will they need a different type of space to sleep?" Once the students decided on which animal to propose, they needed to convince other students. To do this, they used persuasive writing and wrote speeches. The school played the speeches on the school's morning news show. When talking to the students, they seldom noticed the connection between ELA, science, and engineering. Instead, the students focused on how to solve the problem. Callie, a 6th-grader, told students at lunch, "I don't think we should have zoos at all. Instead, I think the zoo should turn into an animal sanctuary. No animal should be born into a cage. The elephants were so big, and now the only animals that would fit are tiny, like the size of dog. It is terrible those elephants lived so long in those small cages." Here you can hear how Callie has learned about the change in space requirements and how this affects the animals in the zoos. She is using this information to convince her peers of these ideas outside the classroom. In classrooms with a high level of discipline integration, students are often able to transfer this knowledge to new contexts, such as conversations in the lunchroom.

Assessment in STEAM Classrooms. A vital piece of any educational model is assessment. It is widely understood that to meet the goals of education, there must be alignment between instruction, learning, and assessment (Biggs, 1993). In a traditional classroom where the goal is for students to learn facts, multiple-choice tests often reflect this alignment. However, in the STEAM model, where the goal is for students to participate in multiple modes of inquiry processes, develop specific skills such as problem solving, and collaborate in various ways, a multiple-choice assessment would represent a misalignment with the authentic, student-driven aspects of STEAM. Therefore, as we developed this conceptual model, we were careful to align the assessment practices to the type of instruction and learning expected to promote STEAM goals.

In authentic assessments, students are asked to apply the knowledge and skills they learned during the instruction and show how they are relevant to the problem they are solving. We define authentic assessment alignment as being connected to the problem the students are answering. For example, in the zoo project, the students needed to be able to calculate the ratio of space to the recommended requirements. They learned about proportions, measurement, and percentages during this project. However, these skills were taught in the context of solving the problem.

To ensure the assessments are linked to STEAM teaching practices, the assessments should be embedded in the learning context. When assessment is embedded throughout the learning process, the teacher provides frequent and high-quality feedback to the student. This embedded assessment serves to enhance student learning by bridging the gap between a student's current understanding of content and the learning objectives. Moreover, it can extend students' learning by encouraging the student to process information in greater depth. In the STEAM unit about the zoo, Ms. Brown held classroom discussions about the difference between abiotic (nonliving) and biotic (living) parts of the ecosystem. Being able to distinguish the two is a state standard, and therefore she wanted to ensure that the students understood the difference. As Ms. Brown states, "Embedded assessments are formative. They tell the students and me where we still need to work."

Though we describe authentic and embedded assessments, we want to be careful not to limit the types of evaluations teachers can design. We feel there are many ways teachers can assess student knowledge, including models, stories, performances, scripts, and designs, among others. The goal should always be that assessments reflect the learning objectives and content standards of the unit.

Learning in STEAM Classrooms

Callie stood outside the lunchroom and passed out flyers that stated, "Vote Sanctuaries Instead of Zoos! Animals' Rights Are Human Rights!" She stopped and talked to a few interested students as they entered the room. Meanwhile, Starr passed out QR codes and asked students to scan the code to learn why the Greenville Zoo should put koalas into the former elephant enclosure. She helped one student download a QR reader, and commented to another student, "They are my favorite animal, too!" Although Callie and Starr took different approaches to solving the zoo's problem, they both learned about life cycles and biomes. However, they learned skills to solve problems—just through different approaches.

During STEAM lessons, teachers support students in the development of skills such as abstracting, analyzing, applying, formulating, collaborating, engaging in argumentation, disseminating evidence, and presenting. The conceptual model looks for teachers to regularly provide opportunities for students to practice these skills in a variety of contexts. Under this model, teachers encourage students to explore multiple paths to solving a problem, which provides favorable conditions for sparking creativity or for exercising creative skills. These creative skills rely on a teacher's ability to offer concepts, tools, and experiences in open-ended problem-solving scenarios. When using this conceptual model, teachers design problems to support student-guided learning. This teacher facilitation relies on peer support and collaboration. By developing issues that urge students to reach out to peers for assistance and work collaboratively, teachers encourage developmentally appropriate levels of social and emotional engagement in learning. In this manner, our STEAM conceptual model is more than just a combination of science, technology, engineering, arts, and math content; it defines an instructional approach by which teachers use a transdisciplinary perspective when teaching about real-world problems.

EXAMINING THE STEAM CONCEPTUAL MODEL ACROSS GRADE LEVELS

This conceptual model plays out differently in various grade levels. Drawing on ways we assisted teachers to implement these instructional strategies across grades K–8, we provide examples of how this model looks different across schools, and also grade levels.

Early Elementary

In one kindergarten classroom, the teacher designed a unit based on the connections between science, social studies, and music. The problem scenario was:

> The average person generates A LOT of trash each day! Over 4 pounds. Where does it all go? Most of it ends up in areas called landfills. At Stone Creek elementary, we are concerned about the amount of garbage in our area, and so we recycle. But what if there are ways to reuse the materials too? Our principal has suggested we create a play space and asked the kindergarten class to help design it. Can you think of ways we can turn the trash into toys?

In this unit, the students practiced problem solving about trash at their playground. The teachers designed this problem scenario with the opportunity to address the different solutions. They allowed the students to brainstorm and then, as a class, investigate the various options together. The kindergarten teachers found that while all the students should be given the opportunity to think about solving the problem in unique ways, in order to support the students during the inquiry phase, there needed to be more guidance. For example, once the brainstorming was complete, the class agreed that creating musical instruments was the best way to use the most trash from the school. The teachers encouraged the students to design their instruments, create songs, and record their music; however, the notion of student-directedness and teacher facilitation looks different in early elementary classrooms. Young students should have opportunities of choice and voice; however, they need guidance in solving the problems, and the teacher noted one way to support students in this learning was to limit the types of pathways the students took. This is an important distinction to make with STEAM teaching across grade levels: The role of the teacher will change according to the content and needs of students.

Upper Elementary

STEAM teaching asks students to engage in multiple practices, and this often plays to the strengths of elementary classrooms as the teachers construct the tasks in a manner that facilitates collaboration and play. However, because of the narrow focus on literacy and mathematical skills, elementary teachers often say that STEAM provides them with a pathway to the other disciplines (science and social studies, typically) through discipline integration. As with early childhood educators, the notion of open inquiry and choice becomes difficult to manage when the teachers are focused on ensuring that their students can read proficiently and have essential mathematical skills. STEAM units in these classrooms often focus more on these content areas, and so the reading shifts to nonfiction to provide the students with content and literacy skills. However, teachers noted that the students seemed more engaged in the text when it was connected to a more significant problem to solve. In Mrs. Davidson's 3rd-grade classroom, the students were examining the school's electricity usage. They read several books on electricity and the sources of power in the area. Mrs. Davidson noted that the students often talked about the readings and referred to them when they created a plan to reduce their energy usage. In this classroom, the students created circuits and investigated different ways electricity can travel. Mrs. Davidson said that she typically was unable to find time to cover this science standard, but through the integrated topics she was able to create this experience for her students.

Middle School

As students get older, they can engage in more complex problems, and therefore it is often easier to provide opportunities for students to participate in multiple questions. In addition, as more middle schools have access to a broader range of technology and types of tools, technology integration becomes more comfortable. Access to technology, along with students' outside experience with technology, often leads to student choice through these tools. In our work, teachers often commented that students had an idea for a different type of technology to help create products, and so the students regularly led this component.

However, the structure of many middle schools creates issues for disciplinary integration. As teachers are content experts in their respective disciplines, discipline integration is often uncomfortable for these teachers. In our work, middle school teachers were able to collaborate with a partner or a teaching team to infuse STEAM across the disciplines. Additionally, we found that in middle schools the art teachers (including music, visual, and performance) were able to assist the teachers in thinking about ways to infuse art into other content areas. In one 6th-grade classroom, students were studying sea level rise through the STEAM scenario that asked them to imagine what the town would be like if there were no beach. The scenario began "Bryson City Council is interested in getting the youth of Bryson Island (BI) involved in their new environmental campaign. They have contacted the 6th grade at BI elementary to be their environmental stewards. As a part of this role, they want to understand this issue and ways to decrease the loss of beach. At the end of this investigation, you will need to focus on one issue and discuss how youth can help eliminate or reduce this problem." The visual arts teacher helped the students create a variety of murals based on this issue, and then create artist statements to discuss the emotional impact of sea level rise. While discipline integration is sometimes more difficult because of the structure of middle schools, there are opportunities for higher-level integration through collaboration.

CONCLUDING THOUGHTS ON THE STEAM CONCEPTUAL MODEL

This chapter provided an overview of the STEAM conceptual model that we developed through our work with teachers. Its goal was to demonstrate how the conceptual model might be applied to instruction by interpreting it in the context of classrooms and guide teachers. Although many of the individual practices assist in student learning, STEAM teaching (e.g., problem-based, teacher facilitation, authentic assessments) involves significant shifts in teaching practice; it takes time to refine and implement effectively. Opportunities for teachers to reflect on their practice while providing support in the context of classroom teaching can help close the gap and move STEAM teaching forward (Dede & Richards, 2012).

CHAPTER 2

Visioning, Planning, and Supporting STEAM Instruction in Schools

This chapter offers ways for schools/districts to build a foundation for STEAM instruction prior to transforming existing schools to STEAM schools or before the construction of a STEAM school. We use an example of how one district provided visioning, planning, and support for STEAM to illustrate the process. We then detail six strategies to consider when building strong STEAM programs. We realize that contexts for schools and districts vary, so we end the chapter with questions and answers for building STEAM programs in unique settings.

VISIONING STEAM

In early September 2016, we received a call from Dr. Gilman, the Chief Academic Officer at a large school district a few hours from Clemson University, where we worked as professors in the College of Education. Our university had sent one-page flyers announcing the STEAM courses and professional development (PD) that we recently began offering to teachers around the state. Dr. Gilman had received this flyer and was curious about ways he might bring STEAM PD to a couple of elementary schools and middle schools in his school district. Two of the schools were being built, and the other two were traditional schools that had existed for decades. All of these schools were slated to rebrand themselves as STEAM schools, a decision made in conjunction with district administrators and each school. Because of this decision, the administrators and teachers had a vested interest in offering their student population STEAM experiences.

However, Dr. Gilman was clear about the fact that the school district was not exactly sure what STEAM instruction entailed and mentioned that they could use help conceptualizing it. During our 30-minute phone conversation, he talked about what he perceived as a variety of great STEAM-related activities students were engaged in during after-school programs that included robotics, coding, and other technology-related activities and community service projects. He also talked about strong ties to the community that a number of the schools had developed over the years and the fact that, as a whole, his teachers were committed to preparing their students at all levels for a future involving collaboration, high-tech careers, and large, global problems to solve. Dr. Gilman explained that, like many districts, theirs drew from a diverse population of students in terms of socioeconomics, race, and culture, and spanned rural, suburban, and urban attendance areas.

Our conversation ended with his asking us to help the district vision and plan for "real" STEAM instruction that could be integrated into daily classroom activities. We chose a date to talk with the administrative team and made a plan to move forward with the community and schools.

This was not the first request we had received to help with STEAM PD. Three years prior to Dr. Gilman's phone call, another large local school district wishing to understand and successfully offer STEAM instruction contacted us to assist them in moving a STEAM initiative forward. Like the district where Dr. Gilman worked, that district was already building a new state-of-the-art STEAM school, but was not sure how to best define STEAM and offer instruction. It also wanted to offer STEAM learning in six other existing schools that were also demographically diverse. We noted two glaring issues often prevalent in well-intended STEAM schools: first, educators and advocates struggle with a clear conceptualization of how STEAM teaching might connect the disciplines (Guyotte et al., 2015; Kim & Kim, 2016; Quigley & Herro, 2016), and second, there is not a one-size-fits-all model for STEAM schools, but instead a model that can be offered and adjusted to meet the needs of the population at hand based on local contexts and relevancy (Herro & Quigley, 2016).

Gilman's district, and the first large district that we worked with, allowed us, over a 5-year period of time, to expand our STEAM PD and research within schools and classrooms to more than 150 K–8 teachers. The teachers were from various grade levels and subject areas, including science, math, English language arts, art, music, and physical education, and began working with us through intensive STEAM PD and follow-up. Nearly half of these teachers allowed us into their classrooms to observe their STEAM teaching in action.

UNDERSTANDING AND DEFINING STEAM

Quickly, we realized that similar to STEM teaching, STEAM is not well understood in the United States. In fact, many school districts struggle to move forward with STEAM instruction, due to issues similar to those recognized in STEM teaching initiatives. That is, many teachers wonder what *is* and what *is not* considered STEAM, and as with STEM instruction, they find it challenging to shift instructional models to support discipline expertise and integrated curriculum (Portz, 2015). At the elementary level, curricula often favor teaching math and literacy over science and technology skills, and secondary school curricula consider each discipline as an academic area, rather than thinking about ways to offer a practical focus that might connect problems to the real world (Williams, 2011).

For STEAM, this has resulted in learning experiences primarily occurring in after-school clubs or informal spaces (Peppler & Bender, 2013), with older learners, with predesigned curricula kits or challenges (Moriwaki et al., 2012; Stevens et al,, 2016), or instruction that has focused on strengthening one or two disciplines or honing programming (Kim & Lee, 2016), art, creativity, and design skills (Tsurusaki, Tzou, Conner, & Guthrie, 2017). While these programs are undeniably important, typically they do not closely align with content and mandated standardized testing to assess the mastery of content, which is likely not their intention or purpose. After-school programs are meant to allow for less rigidity in terms of mandated curriculum and activities. However, this often results in a school approaching STEAM instruction only as an isolated or extracurricular activity that does not include all students or take into account the nature of transdisciplinary problem solving. To move STEAM instruction into the "regular" school day, educators need a sound rationale for why and how integrating various disciplines will lead to quality learning outcomes for students. This can happen, in part, during PD, but before teachers and instructional coaches participate in PD, school districts need to do some groundwork and put supportive structures in place.

In our experience, for schools to be successful in their transition to STEAM education, they need to engage in groundwork that includes visioning and planning for STEAM instruction. And if schools want to incorporate the connected learning model (Ito et al., 2013) as a way to engage and offer equitable participation for students, educators especially need support. Equitable participation is typically defined as fair and reasonable, in a manner that also acknowledges the skills and knowledge students already possess. This background knowledge often comes from cultural norms and family traditions. Considering the fact that the connected learning model relies on interest-driven, peer-supported, academically oriented, production-based, openly networked problem solving with a shared purpose, one can easily see how visioning and planning within the institutional constraints of educational environments, like those posed in schools, is necessary.

BUILDING A FOUNDATION FOR STEAM

Based on our research and success helping move STEAM initiatives forward, we suggest six important actions, detailed below, to carefully consider when building a solid foundation for effective STEAM instruction. First we briefly define and discuss the purpose or rationale for each, and then we offer a plan for how they might be approached. Also, we realize that particular contexts (i.e., rural or urban, diversity and needs of students, capacity to provide resources, parent communities) matter greatly when considering visioning and planning, so we end this chapter with common questions and answers educators ask to provide ideas for how you might address the concerns based on your unique situation. In Chapter 7 we offer additional suggestions for STEAM teaching in different contexts, and in Chapter 8 we discuss overcoming STEAM challenges.

In this section, we discuss the strategies for building a foundation for effective STEAM instruction; these include administrative conceptualization, community visioning workshops, resource assessment, professional development, support structures within schools, and culture and communication.

Administrative Conceptualization

Administrator conceptualization refers to how leaders in school districts understand, define, and provide a vision for STEAM. School administrators, policymakers, and those who control access to resources play an important role in leading and supporting STEAM initiatives, and it is only through a common understanding and vision that this sort of innovation can be successful in school districts.

Administrators and district leaders are charged with responsibilities such as directing academic programs, approving budgets, and shaping state-of-the-art educational environments and programs. STEAM instruction is innovative, but innovating in schools is challenging. Most schools struggle with logistical and infrastructure considerations, curriculum requirements, lack of practitioner understanding, prohibitive policies, and negative attitudes (Collins & Halverson, 2009). Confounding this issue are the short blocks of time teachers are given to shift instruction while juggling various subjects and preparing for standardized tests (Shaffer, 2006). For STEAM programs to have a chance at success and sustainability, administrators and instructional leaders at the district and site level must articulate a clear idea of what STEAM means for the district as a whole, and at individual school sites. This vision should set the tone for the value and promise of supporting STEAM throughout the district and community. Once formed, the vision should be clearly articulated throughout the district. It will impact the type and frequency of STEAM instruction (e.g., Will it be integrated in all K–8 classrooms? Will it be offered monthly, quarterly, or during just one semester?), as well as policies that might be enacted to adjust pacing, scheduling, and resource allocation. Ideally, administrators should consult with experts at universities or existing integrated STEAM schools to better understand what they are undertaking and create a plan of action cognizant of policies, resource allocation, and support structures. Specific ways to reach the goal of offering STEAM

Part II

DEVELOPING STEAM CLASSROOMS

instruction can be refined by individual schools and teaching staff to further meet each site's community needs.

Community Visioning Workshops

Community visioning workshops refer to times for the school and broader community to come together to share in understanding and visioning STEAM instruction.

Often schools wait until instruction is under way before alerting the community about a new initiative through communication from the school board, district, or site. Community-based support is much easier to garner when the broader community has an early understanding of what STEAM instruction might look like in schools. This can be accomplished through brief evening workshops where STEAM is defined, example STEAM units are described, and parents and communities engage in a short STEAM activity aimed at demonstrating what STEAM might look like in a classroom. For example, when we began working with Dr. Gilman, one of our first community visioning days was held in the evening at a local elementary school. We invited the parents, their children, and community members to participate in a short presentation on how the district conceptualized STEAM and their plans to provide PD to all instructional faculty and staff. After describing a STEAM unit centered on finding solutions to eroding local bridges post-hurricane and presenting a problem-solving scenario (further detailed in Chapter 3), those in attendance formed mixed groups. Thus, parents, children, teachers, and a few business leaders all solved a bridge-building challenge together. The school used this activity (see below) during the event to provide the community with an idea of what a portion of an overall STEAM unit would look like. It provided community members with a general idea of how something similar might unfold in classrooms. This scenario was presented to the community:

> In October 2015, Hurricane Joaquin caused major damage to the Low Country in South Carolina. Specifically, it caused the waters to crest at Edisto River (13.64 feet, the highest in 100 years), causing flooding in the surrounding areas. Additionally, the dam at Camp Anderson on Lake Edisto Road failed, which led to the collapse of the bridge on Cleveland Street. Unfortunately, this was one of many bridges to collapse that day. This is a national problem as well. Reports estimate there are more than 8,000 bridges in the nation that are at the risk of collapse. This points to a need to build stronger bridges and look at new ways to build them. The state has hired your team to create a comprehensive plan to address this issue. Therefore, you and your team will be asked to research existing bridges in the areas and new innovative techniques that could be used in places like the Low Country.

and hands-on, and typically less complex). At minimum, during the planning phases, platforms that can easily be accessed and allow for students to collaborate, communicate, and share their work, and that are both developmentally appropriate and interesting to students, should be considered. For instance, if the school district already supports using Google Classroom and associated Google applications, it makes sense to integrate those existing applications into the STEAM unit as a starting point. More complex applications that require unblocking, downloading, updating, or ongoing subscription costs require advance planning and perhaps even training. Finally, if students are allowed to bring their own devices, logistics and permissions for doing so should be planned well in advance.

Technology is not the only, and at times not the primary, resource that needs to be considered. Other important resources that should be assessed and evaluated before STEAM PD and unit planning include student spaces for collaborative work; makerspace tools, including recycled materials, circuits, craft and sewing supplies, or any object that might assist students in figuring out how things work; and outdoor areas (e.g., school gardens, green spaces, rooftop gardens, nearby trails or playgrounds) that might be utilized during the problem-solving process. Distributing or making the resources visible is important. Having a point person to coordinate the resource list and making it easy to access online is the ideal way to plan, assess, and even budget time and resources effectively. We have seen schools handle this effectively through resource teachers, instructional coaches, assistant principals, or even PTO or parent volunteers using Google Drive, websites, or school-sanctioned learning management systems. These online spaces can also serve to share classroom STEAM units and student projects.

Professional Development

Professional development refers to measures taken to help educators conceptualize, plan, develop, implement, and refine STEAM instruction and related units in their classrooms.

In general, for PD to transform practice, it needs to include ongoing feedback, professional learning communities (PLCs), differentiation by subject area, and collaborative opportunities with peers (Skoretz & Childress, 2013). To be effective, PD should not be one-size-fits-all, but should consider the contextual factors that are particular to a local school situation (Clarke & Dede, 2009). It also must be approached as initial training to help conceptualize STEAM instruction and begin developing instructional strategies, and then transferred to ongoing support focused on improving instructional units and practices. Job-embedded PD, in which expertise is located within the context of the schools and then adapted to the constraints and opportunities within the setting, can be particularly effective (Walsh & Backe, 2013). Job-embedded PD means the expert, such as an instructional coach or faculty member, provides PD as needed, on an ongoing basis, at the school site. Professional development could also include a PLC reading a book such as this one and then providing scheduled support with goals and tasks to create and implement STEAM units, with ongoing plans for continued PD through peer review and support from members of the PLC. Because STEAM instruction is approached in a transdisciplinary manner where the problem is foregrounded and the disciplines emerge naturally, there is less need to differentiate subject areas during PD. However, there is a great need to acknowledge and plan for ways the disciplines can be integrated and to identify how schedules might be altered to allow for common planning time, or how classes might be covered by other staff members so teachers can observe one another or provide peer review of STEAM activities.

Quality, ongoing PD is critical to ensure success in teaching and learning, and to that end, PD goes hand-in-hand with support structures within schools, detailed next.

Support Structures Within Schools

Support structures within schools denote the personnel (administrators, instructional coaches, resource teachers, volunteers, or PLCs) in place to help design, implement, and refine STEAM units once teachers engage in PD.

Planning and implementing STEAM instruction is not a small undertaking, especially in the first year of developing units and shifting practice. The realities of day-to-day schooling and standards-based instruction can be particularly daunting if teachers feel they are on their own or unsupported. In some schools, instructional coaches serve as mentors and coordinators to assist teachers in aligning the curriculum with the STEAM conceptual model, more fully developing or refining the units, or even as liaisons to connect community members with expertise to classrooms. In our research, we found that supportive cultures can be created in small school communities that have limited coaching or assistance. This is typically done through schoolwide PLCs, sometimes even including parent and community volunteers, or even accomplished by partnering with local high school classes where older students provide needed support to younger students during design, building, or problem solving. As teachers develop STEAM units, they identify community mentors and experts (see Chapter 3) to assist students in understanding portions of the problem solving or connecting to future STEAM skills or careers. These mentors and experts can assist in offering ongoing support through occasional school visits, email, or video chat.

Culture and Communication

Culture and communication refer to the social behavior, norms, and ongoing dialogue that are cultivated in a school setting to empower educators, professionalize the work, and support transformative initiatives. STEAM education, like any school reform aimed at improving student learning, can flourish and continually improve in professional communities where the culture supports reflective dialogue, opportunities for peer coaching, a strong focus on student learning, and collaboration among teaching staff (Kruse, Louis, & Bryk, 1994). The key to creating a strong professional community with a supportive culture is focusing not on individual teachers, but instead on collectively building a community that educators feel a sense of commitment toward.

Creating a culture of participation (Jenkins et al., 2006) where everyone—students, teachers, families, and the broader community—feels that their contributions matter, and where there are relatively low barriers to entry when producing something meaningful, is the first step to creating a healthy learning culture and professional community. In part, this means that teachers must be able to share their ideas freely and have a hand in setting and reinforcing when and how STEAM instruction will be implemented. Ongoing communication throughout this process is important and should be approached through continual open dialogue with administrators, instructional support, community members, and families to best understand how STEAM instruction is perceived, where it falls short, and what is working effectively. While the initial culture-building for STEAM begins at the school and district site, ideally the culture should be cultivated by bridging a home–school connection where STEAM units include topics and problem-solving techniques based on community relevance and student interests. In essence, the school has to create a culture that involves everyone.

We return to Dr. Gilman's request to have the teachers better understand STEAM instruction through PD. After a few meetings with district leadership to discuss what steps to take in order to support the PD, the leadership team decided on the following plan over a 2-year time period: (1) administrators and instructional coaches came together at the district and site levels to jointly vision and conceptualize STEAM, and shared and refined this vision with their building-level teaching staffs; (2) community visioning workshops were planned for each school, with late-day and evening workshops held for community members and parents; (3) PD was developed and offered over 2 consecutive years to all teaching staff in week-long summer sessions, online during STEAM unit development, and during fall and spring school improvement days; (4) support structures, including instructional coaches, assistant principals, and PLCs, in each school were identified based on the size, availability, and needs of each school; (5) resources were assessed in an ongoing manner during the first 2 years of STEAM instruction, and then beforehand as the district began bringing more schools on board; and (6) the schools built a culture supportive of STEAM education in both their schools and the larger community throughout the process detailed above by sharing what was working well and where they needed additional PD or support. This was accomplished by identifying and bringing in community partners and mentors, continually reflecting on the challenges and finding ways to overcome them, and sharing STEAM units in an online repository for colleagues to revise or get inspiration. The STEAM units were often developed based on student interests, and, as teachers became more comfortable developing the units, they increased opportunities for students to problem-solve based on their interests via topics, technologies, hobbies, and skills.

Finally, we would like to reiterate the importance of visioning STEAM instruction before undertaking a large initiative to transform, build, or create STEAM schools and programs. Reflecting on the STEAM initiative in Dr. Gilman's school district, the administrators, instructional coaches, and teachers changed their approach when extending STEAM instruction to seven additional K–8 schools. Over time, they planned for PD and assessed their resources earlier and made concerted efforts to define and share their vision and expectations at each school site from the onset of the work.

VISIONING AND PLANNING ACROSS GRADE LEVELS

While a common vision is useful when shifting schools to STEAM instruction, there are particular supports that are unique to different grade levels. Here, we outline those supports that support early and upper-elementary teachers as well as middle schools.

Early Elementary

For schools serving early elementary students, it is especially important to involve parents in the visioning phase of planning for STEAM initiatives. Assuring parents that STEAM can include hands-on opportunities to solve problems through play, using guided instruction and whole-class activities, provides parents with a common understanding of the benefits of early STEAM learning. This can be accomplished by including creative expression such as singing, artwork, physical movement, and age-appropriate technologies (e.g., robotics that snap together or use arrows for coding, apps that align with concepts) in problem-solving examples during community visioning workshops. This also provides a strong early basis to build a supportive community. These same ideas about the playful and creative nature of STEAM learning should be incorporated in PD programs with teachers and used as a basis to assess and provide resources.

Upper Elementary

Planning for STEAM instruction for upper-elementary students must acknowledge the ever-widening gap between developmental readiness of individual students, and the typical separation of disciplines that often occurs around 4th grade. As STEAM PD and instructional supports are considered, schools should carefully examine the learning needs of their unique student population. In our experience, it became increasingly important to consider instructional supports for students who struggled with reading or math, or when following multistep directions. For example, one 4th-grade teacher we worked with noted that when the administrative team allocated planning time with special education teachers during the STEAM unit creation and scheduled twice-weekly in-class supports, the entire unit was much more successful and less stressful for both the students and the teachers.

Middle School

The complexity of STEAM units increases as problem scenarios focus on global issues with a local impact, and become more abstract in nature. Fortunately, planning STEAM instruction for older students often increases opportunities to bring in interested community members and mentors to support student learning. We have noticed that community mentors often develop lasting relationships with schools and, at times, particular students. When planning STEAM initiatives, it may make sense to open visioning nights to the entire community, targeting and inviting particular community members to attend. Then, schools can then elicit contact information from interested mentors, and even invite them to brief portions of the PD to help shape the units and confirm schedules.

CONCLUDING THOUGHTS: COMMON QUESTIONS AND ANSWERS ABOUT TRANSITIONING TO STEAM EDUCATION

We end this chapter with comments and questions posed by some members of school communities we have worked with; we include possible solutions, considerations, and potential work-arounds for schools with specialized needs.

What might we do if we have a part-time administrator and/or no instructional coaches? We often see this in rural communities, smaller attendance areas, and schools with declining enrollment. In these cases, it is a good idea to use PLCs and, if possible, draw on community support to help support STEAM units through mentoring, sharing expertise, and gathering necessary resources. One benefit for smaller school populations is the greater ease and possibility of developing school-wide STEAM units where all or most of the teaching staff is involved in co-teaching parts of the unit.

We have very limited resources and technology access. Can we still consider STEAM instructional approaches? While no-tech options make it difficult to implement true STEAM instruction, low-tech options can be used successfully. We have witnessed teachers using work-arounds such as sharing devices, uploading or downloading videos or materials outside of school, or having students access and create content at home or on their personal devices. In terms of limited resources, with a few exceptions in highly impoverished areas, small and large business owners and community members are often very willing to donate materials. Many resources used in STEAM problem solving are recycled or inexpensive. Additional funding through local or national granting agencies is another consideration for underresourced schools. Colleges and universities, if nearby, are also sometimes able to assist in providing resources.

I love the idea of a makerspace, but our school has no physical space to create one. How can we consider this idea? Schools with limited space sometimes repurpose storage closets, dedicate an area of their library/media center, or use makerspace carts that are maintained by parent volunteers, teachers, or students that can be rolled into classrooms during particular learning units.

Most of the caregivers in my school community include working parents or those who struggle with transportation issues. How might we hold visioning days? While each school community has different needs, a few suggestions to include as many parents and families as possible are offering visioning workshops in the evening with child care provided, or during the day as students are showcasing some of their STEAM work, or videoing some of the STEAM problem solving and posting it online with a short explanation to help conceptualize it.

How do we create or find out about PD opportunities? Professional development opportunities will likely present many challenges without planning ahead. As mentioned previously, one option is to develop a PLC using this book and work together to build on-site and job-embedded PD. Another option is to partner with a college or university working on STEAM initiatives. There are some universities that offer online courses or training in STEAM education.

CHAPTER 3

Making STEAM Relevant to Students

This chapter walks you through the basics of creating a useful scenario that serves as the foundation for making STEAM relevant to students. We offer ways to use scenarios as a starting point before fully developing STEAM units, using the STEAM conceptual model to plan learning activities and guide instruction. We discuss how STEAM scenarios and transdisciplinary teaching go hand-in-hand, as the scenarios provide a mechanism to offer transdisciplinary teaching. We then discuss broadening participation with community mentors and experts, since relying on those closely tied to the types of problems detailed in each scenario increases relevance, assists in solving problems, and provides students with a model for potential skills and careers.

EXPLORING MS. ANDRUS'S CLASSROOM

Ms. Andrus projected a music video for her 3rd-grade students to watch, illustrating the waggle dance that honeybees do when communicating with their hivemates to alert them to nearby food sources. Students busily choreographed moves based on the bee's dance they planned to perform as a flash mob at an upcoming STEAM night for their school community. There was nervous excitement in the classroom as the students talked about family and friends who were attending the evening event.

   The students were in the middle of solving a STEAM problem focused on making the community aware of the devastating effects of issues that threatened the honeybee population. The city contracted a local pesticide company to spray for mosquitos, as the mosquitos were carriers of the Zika virus. The company had not alerted local beekeepers, and as a result many of the colonies were destroyed. This destruction of colonies occurred in the students' community, near many streets, neighborhoods, parks, and businesses familiar to them, heightening the urgency to solve the problem. After 20 minutes of developing and practicing their dance moves, the students returned to their groups and logged onto Google Classroom. Ms. Andrus reminded the groups to complete an assignment that involved peer-reviewing one another's group presentations created with Google Draw and now embedded in Google Slides, and to then post feedback. She told them that after morning recess they would head to the school's small makerspace to work on the artificial beehive structures they had designed and built with the help of community mentors and experts.

The STEAM scenario guided their unit, and all of the activities within it. It was neatly written on large poster paper in the back of the classroom as a daily reminder to give their tasks a purpose, and was written in kid-friendly language around the topic of honeybees disappearing in their area. Figure 3.1 shows the unit outline, which includes the problem scenario, driving question, Elements of STEAM, standards aligned to the scenario, brief description of the daily activities, daily outline, resources needed, equipment, experts, and assessments.

Ms. Andrus presented the scenario to the students at the beginning of the unit and used it as part of the hook for students to get them immediately interested in solving the problem. It was also meant to guide the daily STEAM activities. Along with visually presenting the scenario to the students on the first day, Ms. Andrus referred to it throughout the 12-day unit to remind students of the problem they were solving. The problem was purposely open-ended, allowing students to ask new questions and at times taking them down other paths of inquiry, but ultimately all of the students answered the driving question. Ms. Andrus was mindful of remaining relevant to her students as she planned and implemented this STEAM unit. She wanted to provide her students with something they cared about regarding content they might engage with, activities they enjoyed, and a local context they understood.

DESIGNING A STEAM UNIT AROUND INTERESTS

During the unit, Ms. Andrus designed many activities that would lead to solving the problem based on students' interests. For example, she had each group use a digital sketching app to design a section of the school garden that could help increase or maintain the bee population in the area. She knew most of her students were interested in the topic of bees, enjoyed using technology, and loved seeing what other classes had planted in the school garden the previous year. Ms. Andrus spent time getting to know each student, and she surveyed their parents/caregivers at the beginning of the school year to get a better sense of what the students enjoyed, how they learned, and their hobbies in general. Ms. Andrus drew on their interests and designed a locally relevant scenario with hands-on activities.

Getting Students Engaged

Ms. Andrus opened the STEAM unit with an activity to peak their interest. First, she showed a short video of honeybees swarming around a wildflower garden and going back to the hives. Then she presented mini-lessons on using digital design tools and had students collaboratively sketch a model of the garden. Later they would add labels, with planting recommendations, to each section of plants. The students naturally asked questions about why the company sprayed the pesticide and what 1 million honeybees looked like, so she suggested they do research and create graphs to compare bee populations around the country. Once they realized how important honeybees are to the entire food chain, they developed an even deeper interest in what eliminating a vast number of bees from the ecosystem might do to the surrounding community.

Providing Relevant Options to Students

Ms. Andrus gave the students options for how they wanted to present their findings and propose solutions to the problem of preventing colony collapse. She divided students into groups of three or four to collaborate throughout the unit, creating diverse groups in terms of skills and ability levels. Some groups created a honeybee board game with predators, risks, and threats to honeybees and their hives. Other groups made a short video simulating an interview with experts after writing a script and role-playing beekeepers, scientists, and local horticulturists, and all of the students planned a native plant garden based on what would attract honeybees.

We noted how excited and involved the 3rd-graders were in the waggle dance activity, and Ms. Andrus confirmed our thoughts that STEAM could be engaging if student interests were at the forefront of the process. She explained:

> I let students start by designing their native plant garden based on what would attract honeybees. But this was only one part of the problem solving. I gave students choices in how to present their thinking, topics, or solutions to the rest of the class. Sometimes they choose artwork, or create songs or make videos. I have tried to show them how much fun it can be to problem-solve and how they might use technology to collaborate. I even have them think about who might do some of the jobs in the real world.

We saw Ms. Andrus's instruction as a prime example of how making STEAM relevant to young learners can engage and excite them and noted how projects such as these could lead to high levels of learning (Blumenfeld, Kempler, & Krajcik, 2006). Beyond engagement, another reason for using STEAM instruction in classrooms is the value of the problem-solving scenario component: its capacity to facilitate transdisciplinary learning, a primary aim of STEAM instruction (Quigley & Herro, 2016). Although we refer to the problem-solving scenarios as "scenarios" throughout this chapter, teachers should consider the presence of both "problem solving" and a "scenario"

Figure 3.1. 3rd-Grade STEAM Honeybee Garden

Problem scenario:

Honeybees in our area are at risk of becoming extinct! Many people do not realize how important bees are to their lives. Much of the food Americans eat directly or indirectly comes from honeybee pollination. Unfortunately, one-third of the national honeybee population has disappeared over the last 5 years. It is such a problem that scientists have named it "Colony Collapse Disorder," and they asked communities around the United States to participate in Honeybee Health Projects. Recently, Colony Collapse was in the local news because millions of honeybees were accidentally killed in Washington County when a pesticide was sprayed to kill mosquitoes without first warning beekeepers. The cafeteria just informed us that they might not be able to serve some of the school lunches like the yogurt and honey parfait because of the lack of honey available. The bees need your help! As a community of young scientists, you can help by researching this problem and providing solutions to prevent it from spreading, including ways to attract honeybees. With your group, you will create a presentation that Eastside Elementary School's administrative team will view so that they can decide which idea we can safely implement around our school.

Driving Question(s):

How can we attract honeybees and help prevent colony collapse?

Elements of STEAM (i.e., Transdisciplinary Teaching):

Science—how plants and animals depend on each other for survival; which type of plants will attract honeybees and help them to thrive.

Technology—researching different plants for their gardens, designing the garden, graphing, and creating their final presentation to share their solution.

Art—art as design, English Language Arts, drama as students act out honeybee behavior.

Engineering—engineering designs for garden spaces.

Math—measuring the area of the garden to ensure all the plants fit into the garden.

Authentic—how it directly affects the students and how the lack of honey available would impact their lunch choices, including eliminating one of their favorite meals.

Standards:

Math

3. NSBT.1 & 2 Use place value to round whole numbers to the nearest 10 or 100; add and subtract whole numbers to 1,000

3. NSF.1 Develop an understanding of fractions

3. MDA.3 Collect, organize, classify, and interpret data

3. MDA.4 Generate data by measuring to nearest inch, ½ and ¼ inch; organize the data

*Note: NSBT = number sense and base ten; NSF = number sense and fractions; MDA = measurement and data analysis

ELA

Standards 1-4: formulating relevant, self-generated questions based on interests; formulating questions and proposing explanations; constructing knowledge through exploration, collaboration, and analysis; and synthesizing integrated information to share learning

Technology Integration:

Using online research and websites, Google Docs, and iPad apps to create their final presentation (videos, voiceovers, or slides)

Brief Description of Student Activities:

Students will be surveyed before the unit begins so I can adjust activities based on their interests. They will work individually and in groups to research plants that will attract honeybees. Student groups will design a plan for the garden space. They will share their designs and peer-review one another's work, and use the computer programs to design the final presentation. All students will design a garden space; however, solutions and final presentations will vary.

Daily Outline:

This project will last approximately 12 days.

Day 1: Overview of project, show honeybee videos, and visit garden space to measure the area.

Day 2: Expert (garden coordinator) visits class to talk about the garden spaces.

Day 3: Students begin research using resources.

Day 4: Students continue research using resources; invite beekeeper to Skype with students.

Day 5: Students create their own design using the checklist provided; continue research and form groups.

Day 6: Students work in groups to share their designs and provide peer feedback.

Day 7: Student groups create a digital model and begin their final presentations.

Day 8: Student groups begin final designs, offer peer and teacher feedback.

Day 9: Students present projects in a "museum-walk."

Days 10 & 11: Planting days based on discussion of designs, with invited community members and parents.

Day 12: Students reflect on unit, make future plans.

Resources Needed:

Guest speakers, iPads and Chromebooks, teachers and para-educators, planting materials, bookmarked websites

Equipment Needed:

Promethean ActivBoard or SMART Board for class discussions and for final presentations, garden, cubes to measure garden space, iPads/Chromebooks for research and final presentations, software/apps downloaded

Experts:

The Garden Coordinator will come to share garden rules and help students understand plant spacing and what types of flowers can grow in that area. A local beekeeper will visit the class digitally to answer student-generated questions.

Assessment:

Formative assessments will include exit tickets, checklists, observation, check-ins, and content-specific quizzes. The summative assessment will include a criteria sheet and rubric, shared at the beginning of the unit, aligned with the final presentation.

---

for effective STEAM instruction; ostensibly one can exist without the other. Teachers can present problems to solve that are independent of a scenario, and they can present a scenario to guide discussion or activities, similar to real-world cases or moral dilemmas that lack a problem to solve.

Using STEAM Scenarios to Provide Transdisciplinary Teaching

We distinguish the STEAM work we do from other conceptualizations of STEAM by the clear focus on transdisciplinary problem solving (Quigley, Herro, & Jamil, 2017). Developing and presenting students with STEAM scenarios in which there is a problem to solve is the beginning, and heart, of every unit. A well-written scenario provides opportunities to apply transdisciplinary instruction because it foregrounds the problem to be solved, not the discipline (Chapter 4 will explain the role of transdisciplinary teaching in greater detail). The scenarios should be written in a way that is relevant and authentic to students. Relevancy and authenticity mean that the scenario includes an interesting, local, or publicized topic and is developmentally and intellectually appropriate. Additionally, the STEAM conceptual model offers a structure and learning conditions that can help teachers successfully implement each STEAM scenario and an accompanying unit for optimal learning of STEAM concepts.

As discussed in Chapter 1, we use connected learning theory (referred to as "connected learning" throughout this book), described in the work of Ito et al. (2013) as a way to help teachers think about creating transdisciplinary problem-solving scenarios. As a reminder, transdisciplinary teaching involves foregrounding the problem to be solved (i.e., investigating issues around flooding after a hurricane in a local coastal city) versus starting with the disciplines (i.e., providing a math, science, or engineering challenge). Connected learning suggests that a powerful way to engage students is to value their interests and allow them to rely on peers to assist in academic work. Using technology allows for collaboration and networked sharing of ideas, as well as providing a platform for peer review and to connect with a broader community. Furthermore, technology and digital tools are often high-interest areas for students that can be incorporated into the problem-solving process and offer opportunities for creativity and collaboration through game design, video production, digital drawing, and other visualization tools (Grimes & Fields, 2012). Advocates of connected learning remind us that often a mismatch occurs between what students are capable of doing and interested in when considering technology-enhanced learning in schools and strong connections to their interests, peer culture, and academically oriented work (Ito et al., 2013; Jenkins et al., 2006). We believe that a well-designed STEAM unit can provide connected learning opportunities that bridge in- and out-of-school interests and student-preferred practices to promote learning.

CREATING STEAM PROBLEM SCENARIOS

Problem-based learning and scientific inquiry approaches have effectively used scenario-based problem solving for decades as a way to have students contextualize real-world problems and understand scientific processes (Haury, 1993). At the same time, proponents of STEAM believe it is an equitable way to engage and prepare students for 21st-century skills and careers. The approach is equitable, in part, because it favors and contextualizes topics students care about, such as social practices, which emulate concerns in their local community (Guyotte et al., 2015). STEAM also includes ways of learning that students enjoy, such as design, computer graphics, performing arts, creative thinking, and even playful problem solving when exploring and designing solutions (Jolly, 2014). Research that supports using problem- or project-based learning and scientific inquiry (Krajcik et al., 1998), along with early research predicting that STEAM instruction can engage and prepare students, led us to create authentic problem-solving scenarios that involve topics students care about.

Our experience working with and researching STEAM scenario creation with teachers also demonstrated that it is not an easy task. It is challenging because the problem-solving scenarios drive the unit and the associated activities, so they must be broad enough to encompass a variety of activities, but specific enough so students can relate to the problem at hand. Because we focus on ways teachers can teach STEAM during the school day integrated with curricula, versus as an add-on or extra unit, teachers must also align the units with relevant content and standards. There is not a definitive formula to create STEAM scenarios. However, we offer guidelines we have refined through years of practice with teachers to help ensure success.

Begin by Reviewing Content Standards

While starting by reviewing your content standards may appear counter-indicative of many good teaching practices, and many educational researchers argue that standards are often overly prescriptive (Tomlinson, 2000), it is difficult to create and implement a unit if little attention is paid to requisite standards for a particular grade level or subject area. As with planning any good instructional unit, teachers should not simply embed all of their content standards to "cover them." Instead, consider standards that can be met without making the content in the unit feel forced, choosing standards that lend themselves to broad issues or problem solving. Keep in mind that this first step is merely a review of standards.

Standards vary throughout the United States, with some schools and districts focused on the Common Core State Standards, others on specific state-level standards, and others on integrating Next Generation Science Standards in all STEM/STEAM-related units. Here, we focus on the process of creating a scenario; you can customize the standards based on your requirements. For example, if you are a 2nd-grade teacher, during the spring of each school year you might have to meet science, math, social studies and reading standards as follows: (1) science: develop and use models to describe and compare the effects of wind on objects; (2) science: obtain and communicate information about severe weather conditions to explain why certain safety precautions are necessary; (3) math: collect, organize, and represent data with up to four categories using picture graphs and bar graphs with a single-unit scale; (4) math: draw conclusions from t-charts, object graphs, picture graphs, and bar graphs; (5) social studies: identify on a map or globe the location of his or her local community, state, nation, and continent; (6) reading: ask and answer literal and inferential questions to demonstrate understanding of text; use specific details to make inferences and draw conclusions in texts heard or read.

These standards, across disciplines, could easily be incorporated into a weather-related scenario. If you live in the Midwestern United States, your broad topic might be related to tornadoes; if you live in a coastal area, you might consider issues related to hurricanes. Next, you would search for issues that might lend themselves to meeting the standards. Remember, you are just reviewing standards to begin considering a relevant scenario to easily integrate into your daily instruction. The process of selecting standards to meet within the unit is iterative, so you might remove or add standards as the issues begin to crystallize. We find that teachers often begin with a general idea of standards they need to cover during a particular period and make changes as they develop the unit.

One word of caution: The standards and skills must be assessed during the STEAM unit to determine what students have learned and where they need more practice. It is important to choose the standards judiciously. Incorporating more standards does not necessarily mean that the unit will be better, and you do not want to include so many standards that the content feels forced or the unit is overly cumbersome to teach. Finally, if you are a content-area teacher (e.g., primarily responsible for teaching only math or only science or only art), you only need to include and assess the standards you need to meet as you develop your unit. If you partner or collaborate with other content-area specialists, they will include, and assess, their standards within the unit.

Research an Issue Relevant to Your Locale and Connect It to the Standards

For older students, teachers can begin with global issues and connect them to local issues. This approach of moving from global to local is appropriate and is often a preferred way of having students understand the significance of and connection between what happens on a global scale and its impact on their community. Current events, local news and media websites, and national newspapers and radio programs are great places to start. Sources of current events might include digital news found on the *New York Times* website (in particular the science and technology sections are full of relevant issues) or on the *PBS NewsHour* website, Youth Radio, or Ted Talks (there is a playlist devoted to talks for kids). You might scan radio programs such as *Tech Nation, All Things Considered,* and *On Point,* which are all freely available online. For younger students, local news stories that highlight issues in their immediate community are best. For older students, you might consider "hot topics" or current controversial issues.

For instance, as the floating garbage dump became a significant topic student heard on Youth Radio and social media, an elementary teacher we worked with, Mr. Phillips, developed a unit connecting a significant global issue to a local problem by proposing a scenario in which his students were asked to explore how plastic affects the ocean. Mr. Phillips wrote the following scenario:

> You may have heard about the Great Pacific Garbage Patch, but did you know the Atlantic Ocean also has a garbage patch that is approximately 1,014 miles long? Plastics make up the majority of the garbage

in the oceans because they do not biodegrade. The plastics are floating around in the oceans and causing harm to marine life. Just last year a 900-pound leatherback sea turtle that had choked on plastics was found by a fisherman on the North Edisto River. This has prompted Isle of Palms to act to impose a ban on single-use plastic bags and Styrofoam. You can help by joining the efforts of the South Carolina Aquarium in their mission to keep plastics out of the ocean. After investigating the issue with your team, explain how the use of plastics can be harmful to organisms that live in the coastal zone and propose some solutions to this problem to the citizens of our coastal area.

Driving question: How does plastic affect the oceans' environment, and what can we do about it?

In this scenario, a global issue that is also occurring locally, and is relevant to students' lives and interests, can serve as a starting point for the scenario.

Another way to understand salient topics your students care about is to ask them. You can survey or poll older students and talk with younger students about issues of interest to them. For instance, after talking with your 1st-graders, you might note that they are interested in activities in a local park, going to the beach, visiting the zoo, or biking along a newly created bike path, and you can create units around issues related to their environment. Older students might reveal current events they are particularly interested in by reading about them on social media sites or listening to family or peer discussions. For example, Mr. Woods, in the same coastal region discussed above, noticed how often his students talked about an artificial reef the city built from an old bridge. He posed this STEAM scenario to his 7th-grade students:

Creation of artificial reefs off of South Carolina is especially important to the development of our marine fisheries. These human-made underwater structures promote marine life and control erosion, and may even block large ships from passing and doing more damage to ocean life. South Carolina's offshore artificial reefs are constructed from a wide variety of materials ranging from various forms of suitable scrap. Some people suggest that when completed, they can be as beautiful as natural reefs. This project is especially relevant to you, at Prentice Middle School, because the old Route 41 bridge was used to create an offshore reef right off the coast of Charleston. After researching the story behind the new reef and looking at some others in our area, your team will construct a scale model of the actual bridge and present it to Prentice's students and parents. To have others understand what is going on underwater, you will design an activity that demonstrates the marine species surrounding the reef, in this case the bridge, so other students and visitors can learn from you.

Driving question: How do artificial reefs help or harm the development of marine fisheries and contribute to their natural habitat?

Mr. Woods based the scenario, after a review of standards, on something occurring locally that students were already discussing. Ultimately, the fully developed unit with daily activities was co-taught by five middle school teachers and targeted some math, science, social studies, English language arts, and art standards. During their construction and presentation of a scale model of the bridge, which demonstrated their understanding of potential solutions for the problem, the students had many choices in both technologies and materials to use, all based on their interests.

Brainstorm Ways to Integrate Issues with the Standards

It is helpful to collaborate with colleagues to either co-design your STEAM scenario or get feedback for an idea. It is possible to develop a scenario by yourself; however, as with any writing activity, feedback on your ideas is constructive. If you work within Professional Learning Communities (PLCs), you can create schoolwide shared documents with your list of brainstormed ideas and have your colleagues add to them; or, if you have an instructional coach available, your school might set aside ordinary time for coaches to lead activities for the teaching staff to brainstorm and begin the initial scenario-writing. The PLCs can then share the ideas and work together to begin writing the scenario, the next step in creating a STEAM scenario.

For instance, in one elementary school we worked with, the instructional coach, Ms. Rodriguez, set up a shared Google Drive folder organized with grade-level STEAM folders (each teacher implemented two units per year, some co-taught and others implemented individually) and a template for each grade level's STEAM unit (see Figure 3.1 above). Teachers formed PLCs and met face-to-face twice, in the fall and in the spring, to review their standards and scenario ideas, and then provided feedback for one another's ideas in between the two meetings. Some teachers chose to work together to develop a unit, others created their own units—but all received help and support from one another. Ms. Rodriguez coordinated the efforts, uploaded short how-to presentations with scenario-writing tips, and used the common planning spaces on Google Drive as a way to gauge what teachers needed help with or to connect them with community mentors when their STEAM topics and activities were clear.

Write the Scenario in Problem Form

It is essential to ensure that the issue you are building your scenario around has more than one solution and directly asks students to problem-solve. The scenario should also include enough facts or details to get students interested, but not so many that you overwhelm them, lead the students to conclusions, or solve the problem for them. While there is not a mandatory limit for the scenario length, in general, younger students need shorter scenarios that are five to seven sentences in length, while upper elementary and middle school students need more details. It is common for scenarios for older students to encompass two to three paragraphs. The language for all students should be kid-friendly and age-appropriate. Consider this scenario written for an elementary classroom:

> Recently a house fire affected a family at Sawyer Elementary School. Experts think a lightning strike to the house that followed hot, dry weather started the house on fire. We need to understand how the fire occurred so we can take steps to avoid having this happen to someone else. Together we will create and present solutions to help others become aware of what they might do and suggest safety tips. Luckily, the Sawyer Elementary family was not hurt. However, it destroyed all of their belongings inside of their apartment. The family is in significant need of many things they have lost, and have reached out to the school for help. Another job you will have is to work in groups to identify essential items that can be purchased for them from an online website the principal has sent us. Our classroom has a budget of $100.00 that has been supplied by the PTA to present them with things they need.
>
> **Driving question(s):** What can our community do to prevent lightning strikes from starting other fires? How can the Sawyer Elementary School community help people get what they need after a house fire?

The teacher, Ms. Walls, presented the scenario to a 2nd-grade class after news of the fire was in the media, and the school community discussed the impact on the family. Ms. Walls followed the scenario with activities that included investigating weather-related hazards, determining household necessities for replacement items, discussing community resources and support, budgeting and graphing, and creating digital maps with escape routes for their own homes.

In this scenario, the language is straightforward and kid-friendly, some of the activities are completed with the entire class, there is a problem to solve that is identified in the driving questions, and the teacher allows choices for how her students might create and present their solutions.

Write the Driving Question

The driving question is intended to guide the entire unit. Thus, all activities planned within the unit should lend themselves to answering it. This means that the question needs to be essential, or important enough to ask throughout the entire STEAM unit. It also needs to be broad enough not to have one correct answer, but instead a host of solutions that might solve the problem. Most STEAM units include just one driving question, although there are times when two questions might be necessary to guide the unit.

Students may, and often do, ask additional questions that continue to drive multiple lines of inquiry within the larger STEAM scenario. Much of the project-based learning literature distinguishes between essential and driving questions, suggesting that the former is written by the teacher to guide the unit and should then be translated for students so they can develop driving questions of their own (McTighe & Wiggins, 2013). We use driving questions to serve both purposes and suggest that teachers initially write driving questions to "drive" the unit, and then offer opportunities for additional student-driven, "need-to-know" questions that promote additional inquiry. Driving questions should be less directed toward a particular answer and more open-ended (McTighe & Wiggins, 2013). Instead of asking students to describe a phenomenon or asking "what is" or "who are" questions, driving questions often ask, "what we can do" or "how we can" or "in what ways" or "why" something occurs. They should promote higher-order thinking, as they require justification to answer. A few examples of driving questions offered by the Buck Institute (as cited by Miller, 2015) include:

- How have changes in the world impacted native peoples?
- How does probability relate to games?
- Why is science important, and how can it help save people?

We offer a few other driving questions used by teachers we have worked with, including:

- How can we raise awareness of the importance of pollinators through the creation and sharing of a pollinator garden?
- How can simple machines and proportions be used to supply a developing community with sustainable water supply?
- In what ways do artificial reefs help or harm the development of marine fisheries and contribute to their natural habitat?

Finalize the Scenario

Before you are ready to finalize your STEAM scenario and develop the rest of your unit, consider how the scenario might lend itself to particular elements of science, technology, engineering, art, and math. Are there areas of the scenario you can tweak to offer further opportunities for students to explore problem solving through the humanities, art, or math? Is the scenario overly focused on just science and math, with little opportunity to bring in other disciplines through daily activities? Does the scenario get at humanistic problems or social issues that lend themselves to the arts?

As you review your STEAM scenario, note which disciplines are missing, but keep in mind that not all text or tasks within the STEAM scenarios will closely align to science, technology, engineering, art, or math, and forcing a discipline is not a good idea. Students quickly notice when problem solving is unrealistic, and then the tasks become irrelevant to them. Thus, if you are missing some disciplines but infusing them makes the scenario less realistic, do NOT add them in. Another way to consider whether your scenario is on target is to ask yourself, "Do the scenarios presented begin with a problem that naturally draws on many disciplines and would be relevant or interesting to students?" If not, the scenario is probably not appropriate for a STEAM unit and likely not what should be implemented under the guise of STEAM. We mention this because, as we have noted, some teachers want to develop STEAM units by revising prior discipline-focused units. While this practice is acceptable and can be successful for some, it can be difficult for other teachers to move beyond disciplinary teaching, and they often implement a STEM or discipline-focused unit versus a STEAM unit (Quigley & Herro, 2016).

Before you are ready to present the scenario to your students, review the entire problem scenario again. Are there ways to make it more realistic? Are there elements that can be simplified? Is it too long for early elementary students, or too short for upper elementary or middle school students?

We return to the idea that a well-written STEAM scenario lends itself to transdisciplinary teaching that mimics what might happen in the real world, and how real people solve transdisciplinary problems in the real world. Thus, we discuss ways to include community members in STEAM units to help students understand how this work occurs and increase authenticity in the unit.

INVOLVING THE COMMUNITY:
BROADENING PARTICIPATION THROUGH MENTORS AND EXPERTS

After your scenario begins to take shape, you can provide your students with additional relevance by making obvious connections to people who can help them solve the problem. For decades, researchers have studied the importance of involving community-based mentors or experts in students' lives, with promising results concerning students' attitude and effort toward learning, in particular for marginalized youth (Lee & Cramond, 1999). In recent years, educational researchers have talked extensively about the social nature of learning and described how supportive "communities of practice" (Lave & Wenger, 1991) and Internet-based technologies could more easily connect learners to those with expertise (An & Reigeluth, 2011). In both formal and informal, as well as online and face-to-face, environments, community mentoring has been shown to positively impact interest and engagement in learning about new topics, achievement in content areas (Bouillion & Gomez, 2001), and more in-depth understanding about workforce skills and careers.

Although the roles are related, mentors typically work with individuals, groups, or entire classes of students on a regular basis over an extended period, and experts tend to provide shorter informational or problem-solving assistance.

Bringing in experts from the community who solve similar problems, or possess skills that allow students to see why the problem they are solving is essential, connects STEAM to the real world. The inclusion of mentors and experts in STEAM units should not be overlooked, as they are an essential way to provide equitable participation and broaden access for students who might not have opportunities outside of school to people, resources, and imagined futures.

In our STEAM work with teachers, we incorporated mentors and experts in a variety of ways, depending on factors such as the topic, age of the students, availability of the expert(s), and length of the unit. In all instances, the goal is to assist students in problem solving and help them make connections to similar work in the real world.

Choosing Experts

You may decide that one expert is enough to help your students throughout the unit, or that your class would benefit from a combination of experts who might help on a weekly basis, as well as an expert who visits or provides answers to questions that arise as the unit unfolds via email. Depending on the topic your students are exploring, you may choose mentors who are local and can visit your classroom on an ongoing basis, or you may find experts who can visit once or twice either face-to-face or online and videoconference with students on an as-needed basis. In all cases, teachers should identify mentors or experts as the STEAM unit is being developed, with their role noted in the unit plan (see Figure 3.1 above). Typically, teachers identify the general type of mentor or expert they hope to partner with within their unit plan and contact them after the unit is finalized. Some examples of general types of experts that might be noted on STEAM unit plans include a city council member, a factory worker, an environmentalist, a developer, a civil engineer, a politician, a zookeeper, a nurse, an artist, a farmer, and educational outreach specialists from local agencies.

Choosing and planning for community members to share expertise with students can be approached in a variety of ways. Frequently a teacher or staff member knows someone with expertise closely related to the problem outlined in the scenario and contacts them directly. At other times, an instructional coach, resource teachers, or parent volunteers serve as school-community liaisons and assist with identifying and securing mentors and experts.

Using Local Universities and Educational Outreach

For instance, in one classroom a teacher, Ms. Chinn, developed a unit on designing outdoor green spaces with a scenario based on an article on sustainable living in a local newspaper. She contacted a local university's outreach program to find mentors from the university. They, in turn, reached out to industry leaders they worked with within their architectural engineering and education departments, who helped the teachers ensure that the career and workforce components of the STEAM units were relevant and authentic. During the STEAM unit implementation, these same mentors served as guides for the entire class, visiting them in person twice during the 4-week unit and answering questions the students posed as they were problem solving via email and videoconferencing.

Connecting to Nonprofit and Government Agencies

In another circumstance, a group of middle school teachers identified and contacted local nonprofit and government agencies during their STEAM summer professional development after they began developing their unit plans. Math, science, and technology teachers collaboratively created a scenario that asked students to provide potential solutions to an issue involving government officials who were interested in using a local waterway to harvest renewable energy. The scenario suggested that residents were upset about this decision and concerned about the environmental, health, political, social, and economic impact. The students were asked to take on the role of expert scientists and complete some essential tasks: (1) identify, document, and research the problems and alternatives to using this waterway to harness energy; and (2) collect and analyze data regarding the proposed alternative to using the waterway to harness energy.

After the unit unfolded and students conducted some initial research, they traveled with community experts to the local river and surrounding sites to collect data. In this case, community members from local government agencies, such as the city's Director of Parks and Recreation, and experts who worked in sustainable living, soil conservation, and wastewater treatment agencies, served as content-area experts and provided background and evidence regarding the economic, political, social, environmental, and historical considerations of the site.

Partnering with Experts During Professional Development

Another way of approaching connecting mentors and experts with schools and teachers during professional development is to organize an event inviting mentors and experts (we suggest 1 or 2 per STEAM unit) to meet the teachers. Ideally, those conducting the PD should model how the mentors and experts can be used and work with the teachers to identify where in the unit their expertise would be useful. The teacher can match mentors based on the unit topic and their expertise, perhaps pitching potential ideas to teachers and assisting them in creating a problem aligned with the real world—refining the problem scenario the teacher has begun earlier in the professional development. During STEAM unit implementations, mentors or experts can assist the students in the classroom as they are problem solving by answering questions, talking about the skills and careers related to industry and academia, showing how the problem might be addressed in the real world, and providing feedback for the students' final solutions.

Next, we offer a few words specific to grade levels to guide educators to ensure that STEAM is relevant.

MAKING STEAM RELEVANT ACROSS THE GRADE LEVELS

Relevancy is dependent on the students in the classroom. As such, the ways in which the teachers make STEAM relevant will change depending on the students they teach. We found that there are strategies that are useful to particular grade levels. Here, we will describe these strategies across different grade-level bands.

Early Elementary

Early elementary students are naturally very focused on themselves in their immediate surroundings. They also go through periods of intense curiosity about specific topics they observe, read about, or are exposed to (animals, trains, how things work, nature, feelings, etc.). Making STEAM relevant for very young learners means taking a close look at the students' environment, drawing on their interests in specific topics, and then creating a simple, short scenario with multiple activities to practice STEAM skills within the context of their everyday surroundings.

Upper Elementary

Students in upper elementary grades are ready for longer scenarios with added information to explore STEAM problems. They are often very interested in learning about new places, cultures, and traditions; protecting wildlife or the environment; or studying how things work within a system. Making STEAM relevant may involve exploring local issues that can be connected to larger or common issues in other locales.

Middle School

By 5th grade, students can take a more active role in shaping the STEAM scenario used within their classrooms. Global, and even controversial, humanitarian issues may be of great interest to middle school students. And many of these large-scale problems routinely impact students' local communities. As mentioned earlier, surveying or talking with students to discover their interests before developing a STEAM scenario and brainstorming associated problems to solve with them can further shape the STEAM unit and increase relevance for students.

CONCLUDING THOUGHTS ON MAKING STEAM RELEVANT

This chapter introduced you to the idea of making STEAM relevant by developing scenarios that pose local or current problems to solve that are tied to students' interests. Surveying, talking with students and parents, and noting hobbies and topics students often discuss or share with their peers are good ways to find out which topics students care about. Importantly, problem-solving scenarios can also foster transdisciplinary teaching, as they create forums to investigate authentic issues in which the problem is foregrounded and the necessary disciplines to aid in solving the problem emerge through the disciplines. Since the problem-solving scenario guides the learning in the entire unit and provides relevance to engage students, it is important to carefully craft a scenario that makes sense for your locale and the developmental age of your students. Finally, including experts within the unit of study to model how real people use particular skills and assist in solving the problem at hand grounds the problem in the real world and engages students.

CHAPTER 4

Understanding the Role of Teaching Across the Disciplines in STEAM Teaching

This chapter discusses one of the most challenging aspects of STEAM education—transdisciplinary teaching. In this chapter, we explore ways to support teachers to implement the important strategy of discipline integration. We also examine how teachers can align tasks to the problem-solving scenarios to ensure authenticity—another hallmark of transdisciplinary teaching. Finally, this chapter provides examples and strategies to ensure that the STEAM units they create include multiple ways to solve the problem.

TRANSDISCIPLINARY TEACHING AND LEARNING

As discussed in Chapter 3, connecting only the content that helps to solve the problem is a way to achieve transdisciplinary teaching. However, we recognize that the term *transdisciplinary* has been muddled in the education field, as teachers and researchers conflate transdisciplinary with interdisciplinary and multidisciplinary. This conflation creates a misunderstanding when educators attempt to implement these practices.

Multidisciplinary teaching and learning in K–12 happens when students across disciplines work "independently on different aspects of a project"(Mallon & Burnton, 2005, p. 2). Interdisciplinary-structured teaching and learning build upon multidisciplinary teaching, as the goal is to "unify two or more disciplines or to create a new 'interdisciplinary' (hybrid) discipline at the interface of the other disciplines" (Schummer, 2004, p. 11). When we compare multidisciplinary and interdisciplinary teaching and learning to transdisciplinary teaching, transdisciplinary teaching involves multiple subject areas where there are naturally occurring overlapping spaces between the disciplines to produce new ideas (Gibbs, 2015).

When addressing teaching, transdisciplinary learning requires teachers to be able to integrate context while combining a multidisciplinary approach to blending disciplines, or incorporating both context and content integration (Wang et al., 2011). As teachers design STEAM practices, the goal is to implement transdisciplinary teaching. However, we realize that doing so may not always be possible. Using any level of discipline integration provides an opportunity for multiple contents and methods to solve problems. Today's youth will confront challenges and questions requiring a global understanding to solve. The types of questions they will address are deep-seated, transdisciplinary issues, which force comprehensive approaches to problem solving (Galliot et al., 2011).

A truly transdisciplinary space for STEAM education should allow for each discipline within STEAM to occur in concert, making it nearly impossible for students to separate their learning into discrete disciplines (Liao, 2016). This type of authentic integration of subject areas is what we look for in well-designed STEAM scenarios. This transdisciplinary learning in STEAM education is said to have the "potentiality to address contemporary social issues, perhaps even on a global scale" (Guyotte et al., 2015).

This type of problem solving helps students see the connections between multiple disciplines (Pohl, 2005), which is a component of connected learning. When we think of the ways that problems are solved in the real world, or how youth would solve problems outside of school, they would utilize the knowledge they need to solve the problem. Whether that knowledge is math, science, history, or engineering does not matter. Instead, people solve problems using disciplines that are needed. While this might seem obvious, once problem solving is moved into the K–12 sector, teachers often force unnecessary disciplines into their scenarios. Instead, the goal of transdisciplinary teaching is authentic discipline integration. For example, in the problem from Chapter 1 on the zoo enclosures, the math content that the students needed to solve the problem was ratios and calculating area and/or volume. However, understanding animal behavior makes the topic more relevant and provides additional insight to solve the problem.

TRANSDISCIPLINARY TEACHING IN ACTION

Mr. Dando introduced a STEAM problem with a video of Hurricane Harvey landing in Houston, Texas, followed by another video of Hurricane Irma rushing onto the shores of Charleston, South Carolina. After the two videos, he asked the students in his 8th-grade science class to explore the reasons for the difference in the amount of flooding. "Why did the flooding devastate Houston, but Charleston was able to recover quickly from the hurricane? Discuss this with your tablemates and see if you have any initial ideas." The low roar of animated conversation began as the students brainstormed ideas together at their lab desks.

"Maybe Harvey was a stronger storm?" one student, Gabby, suggested. Her group member, Brian, began looking up the severity of the two storms on his smartphone, reading facts about wind speed and amount of rainfall. Nick, their third group member, peered over Brian's shoulder and reminded the group, "Houston isn't used to flooding like Charleston is. Have you been in Charleston when it rains? It always floods and then like 3 hours later everything is fine. It is probably related to the way the city was built."

Using a transdisciplinary approach, an approach that begins with a real-world problem and naturally integrates the disciplines, Mr. Dando introduced the students to topics of flooding, weather, and engineering design in the following STEAM problem scenario:

> You may remember hearing about the severe flooding in Houston after Hurricane Harvey. The reason areas around cities flood are usually due to a design problem where water comes in, but it cannot quickly move out. Engineers have been working on ways to solve this problem for centuries. The ancient world has had amazing engineering feats with the movement of water, such as the shadufs and canals in the Nile River Valley, the wells in the Indus Valley and Greek city-states, and the aqueducts in ancient Rome. The elaborate water systems included the use of simple machines that were efficient. You are a developer who is working with the city to design and engineer the movement of water to a developing community just outside of Charleston. You will work with a team to solve this problem (using your knowledge of simple machines) so water moves to adequately sustain your developing community.
>
> **Driving Question(s):** How can simple machines and proportions be used to supply a developing community with sustainable water supply? How can the ancient world lend knowledge to solving this problem?

Here, the students examined how water is a vital source that influences many aspects of life, including architecture. By designing the curricula around the problem, Mr. Dando attended to one of the tenets of STEAM education—transdisciplinary teaching. In the STEAM conceptual model, we examine different levels of discipline integration occurring during instruction, with the ultimate goal of teaching in a transdisciplinary manner. To do this, we work with teachers using a transdisciplinary approach *from the beginning of the curricular design,* as Mr. Dando did. When teachers focus on this approach while constructing the problem scenario, it becomes less daunting than if they attempt to add transdisciplinary approaches after forming the scenario.

Transdisciplinary teaching begins with a problem the students will solve and integrates the disciplines that are naturally used to solve the problems. In Mr. Dando's classroom, he ensured the problem was the central focus of the STEAM unit and aligned the content to the problem. To do this, he used standards to guide the planning, but the implementation of the approach included focusing on the issue of developing a water supply and alignment of other content (math, social studies, ELA, engineering) areas outside of his content area, science. Specifically, he aligned the problem to the science standards he taught (weather, climate change) but recognized when implementing STEAM curricula that to be transdisciplinary, the unit should focus on a real-world, relevant problem for the students to solve. To accomplish this, he also integrated other disciplines. He found this relatively easy to do because he recognized that adding in other subject areas, such as math, mimics the way people address problems in the real world.

What makes transdisciplinary learning important for problem solving is the focus on the content of one discipline with contexts from a different subject to make the content more relevant. In Mr. Dando's classroom, the science content was simple machines. However, situating it in a problem about flooding, and understanding how some cities are more or less likely to flood, provided a platform for solving the problem. When the teaching team decided to integrate the social studies standards about the ancient world, they recognized that if scientists and architects were solving this problem, they would look to history for previous successes to understand how to solve future problems. Additionally, using evidence and claims was a part of this problem solving (ELA standards). This way, the teachers planned a STEAM problem scenario that mirrored the problem-solving process.

CONNECTION TO COMPONENTS OF THE STEAM CONCEPTUAL MODEL

The STEAM conceptual model focuses on how transdisciplinary teaching can support the components within the model, including discipline integration, authentic tasks, and multiple ways to solve the problem. In this chapter, we focus on how transdisciplinary teaching can create a classroom environment including these strategies.

When teachers begin designing the transdisciplinary aspects of STEAM units, they are often concerned about meeting standards. In our view, transdisciplinary teaching does not have to be counter to standards. In fact, in the classrooms we observe, transdisciplinary approaches often help teachers design units that can connect standards in meaningful ways. During unit design, we recommend that teachers begin with their standards and focus on a problem that is aligned with the standards to create the problem scenario. In Mr. Dando's case, he previously designed a simple machines unit where he tasked the students with building a machine that carried a specific load. In this unit, the students solved a problem, but it lacked the real-world context. For Mr. Dando, this was a good starting point, and we have found similar experiences with other teachers. Many of them have done some problem-based instruction or offered "challeng-es" for their students. Sometimes this is an entrance to STEAM; however, it needs to ensure that the disciplines are connected, the tasks are authentic (relevant to the students' lives and the problem), and there are multiple ways to solve the problem. Because Mr. Dando works in a middle school with a team of teachers in disciplines including math, English language arts, and social studies, they co-planned this unit. The initial focus of this unit was the engineering design principles through the design of the aque-ducts or wells. This initial focus on engineering design principles ground-ed the unit, and the other disciplines supported this focus. In Figure 4.1, we provide a description of how the standards and the activity align to meet the standards. The table includes science, technology, engineering, art, math, social studies, and ELA standards. In the bullets following each standard is an example activity that the teacher designed to align with the corresponding standard.

AUTHENTIC DISCIPLINE INTEGRATION

One of the components of the STEAM conceptual model ensuring trans-disciplinary teaching is authentic discipline integration. This authenticity means ensuring that the content areas that were aligned during the instruc-tional planning were naturally aligned and not forced into the unit to cover more standards. When teachers attempted to force in content areas that would not be typically used to solve the problem, the students noticed this inauthentic inclusion, and they often became disengaged from the problem, commenting, "This just feels like school again." For example, in Mr. Dan-do's classroom, in one of the lessons, he asked the students to review all the types of surface changes that occur during earthquakes (i.e., sublimation) without connecting it to the problem scenario. The students became frus-trated, as they could not see the connection to the problem. In fact, one stu-dent stated, "No, this isn't how you would solve the problem. Memorizing the types of surface changes is just something we have to learn because it is in the standards." When we discussed this with Mr. Dando, we talked about several options to help with the authentic integration of science content. First, he could keep the standards related to the Earth's surface changes, but he would need to construct a lesson to help the students understand how different changes in the Earth cause various issues. For example, some of the students could examine how the impact would have been different if an earthquake caused a tsunami versus a hurricane. The second option was to remove the earthquake lesson from this unit and integrate it into a different unit altogether. Ultimately, Mr. Dando decided to remove the earthquake lesson from his unit plan and focus on the issue of flooding after a hurricane. This change in instructional planning helped to ensure that the

Figure 4.1. Standard Alignment to STEAM Problem

Science Standard:

Design and test solutions that improve the efficiency of a machine by reducing the input energy (effort) or the amount of energy transferred to the surrounding environment as it moves an object.

- Design the aqueducts/wells with the use of simple machines.

Technology Standard:

Critically curate a variety of resources using digital tools to construct knowledge, produce creative artifacts, and make meaningful learning experiences for themselves and others.

- Create a proposal to be presented to the town council.

Engineering Standard:

Plan and conduct controlled scientific investigations to provide evidence for how the design of simple machines (including levers, pulleys, and inclined planes) helps transfer mechanical energy by reducing the amount of force required to do work.

- Engineer the aqueducts or well systems.

Art Standard:

Generate and conceptualize artistic ideas and work.

- Research how civilizations have used water sources as design and incorporated them into their architecture.
- Create the aesthetically pleasing (beauty that inspires emotion) design for the modern-day fountain.

Mathematics Standard:

Apply the concepts of ratios and rates to solve real-world and mathematical problems.

- Determine the actual amount or capacity of water necessary to allow for the aqueduct to properly function as a drainage system for disposal of waste and garbage.

Social Studies Standard:

Demonstrate an understanding of life in ancient civilizations and their contributions to the modern world.

- Consider Charleston's failed solutions to access clean water; then look to other civilizations such as ancient Rome, a city that built an empire based on water, to research more efficient ways to consider engineering an efficient and beautiful model for accessing clean water.

English Language Arts Standard:

Trace and evaluate the argument and specific claims, distinguishing claims that are supported by reasons and evidence from claims that are not.

- Create a proposal persuading the town council to use your design.

transdisciplinary STEAM problem scenario maintained the authentic integration of disciplines needed to solve a problem.

It is the transdisciplinary approaches in the context of STEAM education that offer students the holistic and problem-based learning opportunities they need to be successful in their future careers. These educational practices are thought to provide an authentic method of subject integration rather than simply adding all subjects together into one lesson for the sake of doing so.

Conceptualization of Transdisciplinary STEAM Education

In our research, we found STEAM teaching should position teachers to create transdisciplinary problem-solving scenarios foregrounding problems for students to solve, using creative and collaborative skills that encompass various disciplines. Beginning with a problem to solve is markedly different from beginning with the discipline or content and having students solve narrow problems (Herro & Quigley, 2016). To illustrate the difference between the two approaches, we provide the examples below:

Transdisciplinary STEAM Scenario Example:

In May 2016, 35-year-old Tonya arrived at the emergency room at Mary Black Hospital after complaining of a headache, some muscle pain, and fever. Tonya arrived with a slight fever (101°F) and a severe case of conjunctivitis (pinkeye). Doctors noted she had returned from a family vacation in Puerto Rico 3 days earlier, where she reported reading on the beach most days, eating at the hotel and local restaurants, and going on a snorkeling excursion. She had three noticeable mosquito bites. After running some blood tests to confirm their suspicions, doctors diagnosed Tonya with a mosquito-borne infection.

Mosquitoes are the deadliest creatures on earth, leading to the death of over 1 million people each year just through transmission of malaria. Although malaria no longer exists in the United States, new mosquito-borne diseases such as West Nile virus, dengue, Zika, and Chikungunya have arrived. No vaccine or specific treatment exists for any of these illnesses. As such, prevention is essential, and health organizations are searching for ways to target and control problem mosquito populations.

You are a member of a group working for the CDC assigned to identify Tonya's mosquito-borne illness and identify ways to control the spread and transmission of a virus. To propose a solution, you must consider numerous issues. Some of the problems include mosquito habitat, life cycle, and ecology; efficiency of virus transmission and persistence within the mosquito population; efficacy of current and new mosquito prevention technologies; ecological impacts of reducing and/or eliminating mosquitoes; and risk assessment of the case, social and economic effects of travel bans to infected countries, and the likelihood that Tonya's infection may lead to an epidemic. You will present your proposal to the Secretary of Health and Human Services and her department. It should include evidence that multiple ideas were carefully examined to propose a solution in the best interests of the general population.

Discipline-Focused Teaching Example:

Explain how mosquitoes transmit diseases. Compare and contrast the diseases, discussing the difference between bacteria and virus transmission.

The differences between the approaches are that STEAM teaching:

(1) addresses problem solving through a real-world application in which there is not a definite answer (e.g., the students are asked to identify Tonya's mosquito-borne illness and identify ways to control the spread and transmission of the virus.

(2) multiple disciplines are acknowledged in that the scenario incorporates the use of several disciplines, such as engineering practices in determining the virus efficiency and technological advancements; English language arts (ELA) during the communication of evidence as well as persuasive essay-writing during the formation of final ideas; science concepts during the investigations on viruses, transmission rates, and understanding the human body systems that are affected; technology through the use of visualization tools (e.g., Google Maps to see rates of infections) or videos (e.g., iMovie); social studies through exploring which countries are successfully battling these diseases and why (e.g., there is evidence that certain climates and geological landforms are more prone to Zika); and the creative arts through creating music evoking the feelings of contracting a disease or writing a poem about emotions that arise during an outbreak.

(3) requires collaborative skills to present a solution as the students are placed in teams to solve the problem. When contrasting the transdisciplinary approach to the discipline-focused approach, the latter relies heavily on science standards to have students explore a problem with a goal of

producing the same answer. One might argue that the former is a more authentic teaching and learning approach, as we anticipate students encountering new questions as they become curious about why certain people and countries are at greater risk, what the gender bias is for certain diseases, and the technologies available to control mosquito growth.

Connection to Connected Learning

Another promising aspect of providing transdisciplinary STEAM problem solving is that it offers opportunities for connected learning. Creating transdisciplinary problems to solve that students care about provides a forum for interest-driven, academically oriented, production-centered work. In our research, when the teachers connected the ideas from multiple content areas to the problem solving, the students saw how the skills and knowledge learned from one content area related to solving the problem outside of a specific one.

In another classroom, the 5th-grade teaching team developed a unit with the following STEAM problem scenario:

> *Condé Nast Traveler* and *Travel and Leisure* magazine just named Charleston, South Carolina, the world's best city. This impressive ranking is attributed to the arts, dining, shopping, and rich history of this great American city. South Carolina coastal cities are among the fastest-growing in the nation. While Charleston can be very proud of its ability to attract people to visit and live in the area, this honor also comes with some consequences for the city. The area faces the challenge of growing at an average daily rate of 45 people per day. Rapid population growth can create a plethora of issues and problems, like repairs for big-ticket road projects, lack of parking issues, overcrowded beaches, and the need for new schools. For example, in Berkeley County School District, the district plans to add three new schools each year! One particular area of focus is to determine what is best for residents and the community, including easing traffic congestion and facilitating faster commutes with safety and procedures. However, there are many other concerns. The tri-county government is interested in learning about ways other cities have dealt with these issues and have asked for your help in deciding what the most important issue is. You and your team will research and determine which area the government should focus on (e.g., environmental issues, social services, tourism, education, traffic plans). At the end of this investigation, you will create a proposal for the government to review as well as a persuasive infomercial trying to convince them to choose your area.

In this example, the 5th-grade teachers planned a unit beginning with this problem for the students to solve: to investigate the challenges of population growth in the area. This problem integrates disciplines, as all students researched a variety of topics before choosing their area of focus, and then created a persuasive essay before their infomercial. The students also utilized technology integration during their moviemaking process (they used iMovie).

During the investigations, the students discovered that many of these challenges were occurring because of another factor not mentioned in the problem scenario: climate change. Their county is in what is called the Low Country and is below sea level. This causes many issues related to flooding. The increased number of hurricanes due to the temperature and sea level rise of the ocean has increased the frequency and severity of flooding.

When creating authentic STEAM problems from a transdisciplinary perspective, one of the benefits and challenges is that students end up going down investigatory paths that are different from those the teacher intended. In this classroom, the teacher, Ms. Jones, encouraged this, but she had to be flexible with her daily plans. One of the outcomes of transdisciplinary curricula is that it does not position one discipline over another—the methods used to solve the problem can be as varied as the disciplines studied. When discussing this with the teachers, they stated that while initially this changed the timeline of their project, they took a look at their yearlong pacing and realized that "impacts on the environment due to humans" was to be studied later in the year. Therefore, they incorporated those standards into this unit, which provided them with more time to focus on this unit. In this way, the flexibility the teachers had with the curriculum guides permitted transdisciplinary learning. Another deviation from the curricula occurred when several students discovered that, similar to many cities across the United States, when the population increases there was an initial tax on the healthcare industry. They found that this was already an issue for their area, and the students began to research why. Similar to when the students directed the learning about climate change, the teachers used this as an opportunity to investigate the historical shortages in social services and how these shortages impact the economy. They were able to connect this to the social studies standards in regard to Reconstruction, which state, "Reconstruction was a period of great hope, an incredible change, and efforts at rebuilding. To understand Reconstruction and race relations in the United States, the student will compare the political, economic, and social effects of Reconstruction on different populations in the South and in other regions of the United States" (South Carolina Department of Education, 2011). In this way, Ms. Jones used this unit as an opportunity to discuss what happens when cities change; there are often issues related to access to social services, and at times to race.

Our view of transdisciplinary teaching focuses on problems that are content-based, and authentically so. When teachers create a scenario that is situated in an authentic problem, there are natural connections between the disciplines (here, persuasion, but also history and science). Through our conceptualization of STEAM as transdisciplinary, the goal is not to check off all the boxes of science, technology, engineering, arts, and mathematics. The goal is to find those disciplines that are naturally used to solve the problem and provide a pathway for discipline integration instead of forcing *all* the subjects into the problem scenario.

CONNECTION TO AUTHENTIC TASKS

As we've mentioned previously, when the problem scenario is transdisciplinary, the disciplines aligned should support the problem solving. As a result, it is crucial for teachers to ensure that the tasks the students do during the STEAM unit align with the problem they are solving. This alignment of tasks to the problem means that as teachers plan, they should consider what they have the students do to support the problem solving, or authentic tasks. The tasks should assist in solving the problem. In one 1st-grade classroom, the teacher, Ms. Ansel, designed a STEAM problem scenario around the topic of air pollution:

> According to the *Post and Courier* newspaper, the Charleston area population is growing fast, with an average of 45 people a day moving here. With the growing population, there is more air pollution. The air pollution from cars and factories can make it hard for people and plants to live. You and your partners will figure out the ways the increasing population in the around us affect where we live. Can you think of ways to solve this problem?

The STEAM problem scenario is problem-based because students are trying to discover the effects of an increasing population. Ms. Ansel carefully designed the daily tasks to help the students solve the problem. To make the unit both age-appropriate and manageable, each group choose an area to work on—one group chose a paper plant, another chose an electric utility plant, one housing, and the last group chose transportation to figure out the different ways increasing the population would affect their town. During one lesson, the entire class created a physical model of the city, named Danger Town, with examples of how their chosen topic (housing, transportation, etc.) would be affected by increased population and what that would do to the city (see Figure 4.2). The spaces were connected with a track to depict a person traveling through the day and experiencing these issues. Ms. Ansel integrated technology throughout this unit, but in this lesson, she specifically incorporated the use of Ozobots, which are small robots controlled by coding them to make movements. The Ozobot simulated a person traveling through the day and their experiences if they encountered these different

Figure 4.2. Student-Designed "Danger Town" to Describe Cause and Effect of Air Pollution

places. One group was researching the paper plant and during the discussion of the causes and effects of the plant coded their Ozobot to "back walk" and "slow" because "the plant cuts down trees to turn it into paper and burns it. And the plant adds chemicals. The chemicals and the smoke come out to the air. When the Ozobot gets there, the smoke makes it walk backward and slow down because it is hard to breathe."

In this example, the teacher connected the students' tasks to solving the larger STEAM scenario of how increasing population would affect their area. For example, the tasks such as researching a topic, creating a model, compiling their ideas into one large model, discussing the causes and effects of their issue, and coding the Ozobot to simulate changes in the environment helped them solve the problem. Because they were related to solving the problem, they were authentic tasks, meaning that these are things that would help to solve the problem, but also they are tasks that are similar to those done in the real world if experts are trying to solve this problem. Experts would focus on a variety of issues, create models, and simulate changes within those models.

Often authentic tasks are difficult for teachers to design in STEAM teaching. At times, we witness teachers who have designed a problem-based, transdisciplinary, and relevant STEAM scenario, but then the enactment falls short. They resort to what they would typically do and lose sight of the problem the students should be solving. One technique to remedy this issue is to circle back to the problem as teachers design their daily lessons. We suggest asking the question, "Does this task help them understand or solve the problem?" If it does, then it is an authentic task. If it does not, we suggest reworking the task to ensure that it will help solve the problem.

A PATHWAY FOR MULTIPLE METHODS TO SOLVE THE PROBLEM

One of the goals of both STEAM education and connected learning is to create an opportunity to engage *all* students in learning. For example, when examining STEAM teaching practices, we found it critical to support multiple methods to solve the problem, not to privilege one way of knowing or doing. Therefore, an instructional strategy supporting various ways to address an issue is one that invites participation from students.

When examining whether lessons promoted finding multiple solutions to a problem, teachers must consider whether the problem supports future questioning. By ensuring that the problem allows for future questioning, the problem can change slightly as the students progress through the task.

One of the schools we worked with decided to do a schoolwide implementation of a STEAM unit. Its region had experienced a hurricane, and the town flooded. The city used the school as an evacuation point, and therefore the children had strong memories of their school's role in helping the community rebuild. Each grade level had slightly different versions of the problem scenario. The 4th-grade teaching team designed the following:

> On October 1, 2015, our area experienced a large amount of rain due to a stalled storm offshore. The area received 15–25 inches of rain within 48 hours. This amount of rain caused a substantial amount of flooding and damage in our community and forced many community members to evacuate from their homes. The National Guard was called in to help rescue people, and our elementary was even used as a shelter-in-place during this time. Houses were not constructed to withstand a storm of this magnitude, so nearly a year later, families and community helpers are continuing to rebuild their homes and restore their property. Specifically, what type of preventive measures or steps could our community members take to protect and reduce the impact in the future? What kind of effect could severe weather conditions have on their homes and their families?

The team designed a unit including a real-world problem to be solved and opportunities for discipline integration, and the specific question was open-ended, which allowed students to investigate multiple paths. However, during the observations, we noted that the teachers led the students to one specific way to solve the problem. Instead of investigating ways to reduce the impacts on communities during floods, the students were asked to "choose a type of severe weather." Then the students recorded their research on a teacher-created template. This template included specific facts such as "characteristics of the severe weather," "definition," "frequency," "the region(s) where their type of weather is most prevalent," and to "identify appropriate tools used to measure data, for example: anemometer, rain gauge, wind vane, or thermometer." The teacher asked the students to keep track of their references, and then create a brochure about their severe weather type.

While creating an educational brochure undoubtedly involves other disciplines (ELA in research and writing, technology in creating a digital booklet, science while learning about the weather), the connection to solving the problem was missing. Although brochures could help people become aware of the weather and therefore prepare, the types of facts students were asked to include were narrow and specific. At the end of the unit, the student-designed brochures looked very similar across all the severe weather types. Solving this problem in this way did not encourage multiple ways to solve the problem. More specifically, the students did not solve the problem of "What type of preventive measures or steps could our community members take to protect and reduce the impact in the future?" Instead, they created a list of facts about weather types.

Unlike the previous example of Ms. Ansel's classroom, the students did not investigate unintended paths. In this way, the curriculum was teacher-directed and did not foster opportunities for students to follow their interest. While this problem is relevant to the students' lives, the *way* the problem scenario was enacted prohibited the implementation of multiple methods to solve the problem. What is interesting about this school is that the teachers had the support of the principal. The principal was flexible with the pacing and curriculum maps. For example, the entire school was investigating this STEAM scenario, and there were opportunities to rework the pacing guides. In fact, the principal requested the pacing guides shift to meet the needs of STEAM education. However, the teacher in this example still felt the need to be in control of the curricula.

Many STEAM teachers discuss multiple solutions to the problem as a challenge. One teacher put it well when she described her middle school math classroom. "I am so impressed with the different directions the students are taking this project. I am excited about their creativity and to see how their strengths and interests show up in their work. However, it is still really hard for me to loosen up with my plans. I am getting better, but the pressure of 'keeping up' with the pacing is really hard to let go. Even when I know, we are covering enough standards and doing actual problem solving. It is just tough to let go." Here, we recognize the tension between authentic learning, student engagement, and multiple paths and the time-lines of the pacing guides. This tension suggests that even with school supports teachers need specific strategies to become better at facilitating learning and to become flexible in their teaching plans to foster multiple ways to solve a problem.

STRATEGIES TO SUPPORT TRANSDISCIPLINARY TEACHING

During Mr. Dando's instructional planning, he noted that there were several strategies that aided in the transdisciplinary design of his STEAM unit. These included a strong understanding of what STEAM education is and feedback during the curricular design process.

Conceptualizing STEAM

Being able to conceptualize a new educational practice is a crucial component to successful implementation of that practice (Herro & Quigley, 2016). Despite some background in or STEAM training by at least half of the participants with whom we worked, most had limited understanding of STEAM as including transdisciplinary approaches. They viewed STEAM as addressing, but not necessarily integrating, multiple disciplines. This lack of integration led to "ticking off the individual disciplines," as one assistant principal noted. We found this consistent with Son et al. (2012), suggesting that teachers may understand core concepts of STEAM but struggle to articulate it in theory, much less enactment. While many teachers had a conceptual understanding of how to include the arts and humanities as part of transdisciplinary teaching, they primarily considered media arts as focused on creative ways to deliver final products. This focus on final products points to the need to have teacher educators involve arts and humanities experts in PD efforts and the curricular design process. The teachers had difficulty moving from inter- or multidisciplinary teaching toward transdisciplinary as a way to frame the problem solving. That said, one strategy that assisted in better conceptualization of transdisciplinary thinking was collaboration. There are two ways in which collaboration helped the teachers with transdisciplinary thinking. First, they believed in collaboration by incorporating other disciplines into their teaching (e.g., science teachers considering mathematical concepts). Second, collaboration helped them identify areas where they would need content expertise outside of their specific disciplines. Because STEAM requires teachers to incorporate multiple content areas, the teachers felt that this type of collaboration provided them with the necessary support to integrate various content areas and modes of inquiry.

Supporting Curricular Design

The other area that led to the success or difficulty of transdisciplinary STEAM teaching was the curricular design component. While the teachers we worked with were able to develop a STEAM problem scenario, the levels of incorporation of relevance to the students' lives and the degree to which it was problem-based varied. At times, teachers had a project in mind that they wanted to tweak to make it "STEAM-like." For example, if they had previously created a unit where students made a model of a plant cell, they were often focused on including that project in their unit. We found that this was often very difficult for teachers to do, as it would likely be irrelevant to the students' lives or be so focused on a product that it was difficult to add in a problem-solving component.

That said, we found that even for teachers who had a solid conceptualization of transdisciplinary teaching in STEAM, they were often intent on doing a specific project. For these teachers, we usually asked them to refer back to their standards and their long-range pacing guide to map out the breadth of the concepts students should learn in their class. With a variety of topics in mind, we were able to help them to see the connections to the real world. Not surprisingly, this was often the most difficult part of the curriculum design process. Several supports increased the teachers' ability to do this. The first was time dedicated during the PD to allow the teachers to brainstorm, draft a problem scenario, and collaborate with their colleagues. Teachers note that during the school year, there is very little time to draft these innovative STEAM problem scenarios. The second support was feedback from the authors and their peers. This feedback helped to refine the problem scenarios, which often needed more explicit connection to real-world problem solving and ensuring that there were not disciplines forced into the problem scenario that would make it inauthentic. The last support that increased the likelihood of transdisciplinarity in the curricular design was flexibility with the pacing guide. If teachers were able to move topics around in the pacing guide, they were able to create more authentic problem scenarios that involved more subject areas. We found in our work that most districts were flexible with the pacing guide; however, in one instance a district was unwilling to allow this flexibility, which restricted the teachers' ability to move beyond multidisciplinary curricular design in most cases.

TRANSDISCIPLINARY TEACHING ACROSS THE GRADE LEVELS

Because we view transdisciplinary teaching as beginning with a relevant real-world program that authentically integrates disciplines, this will look different across the grade levels, as curricular design shapes this process.

However, we found that transdisciplinary teaching can be achieved irrespective of grade level.

Early Elementary

In early elementary, where teachers regularly teach a variety of subjects, teachers readily achieved transdisciplinary design. However, the challenge was ensuring that the problem was open-ended enough that there could be more than one solution. It can be challenging to ensure that the problem is not too complex for early learners to solve. In a 1st-grade classroom, the students investigated an issue about the harmful effects of the sun. During the STEAM unit, the teachers provided initial ideas about the effects of the sun but encouraged students to think of others. In this example, students are not forced down one pathway but rather are encouraged to bring in their perspectives and experiences to solve this problem.

Upper Elementary

In upper elementary, where teachers often begin specializing in content areas, ensuring transdisciplinary teaching through discipline integration, authentic tasks, and multiple methods is often about horizontal alignment with their standards. Because teachers often teach only one content area, there needs to be time to look across the standards they teach to understand where there could be discipline integration that would be related to a real-world problem. For example, a 4th-grade teacher, Ms. Smith, who taught ELA and science, aligned the science topic of sound and the ELA topic of developing a plan to take informed action in a problem to assist students in their school with auditory-sensory disorders. The goal was to create settings where these students could more readily participate in an inclusive environment. While Ms. Smith did not teach math, she worked with her teaching partner who taught this subject to create a budget for their solutions.

Middle School

In middle school, the challenges teachers face often are related to the school structures. If teachers were not a part of a grade-level teaching team (meaning that multiple content areas such as math, science, SS, and ELA plan together), they felt that their opportunities were limited to the content area they taught. That said, we observed teachers who were able to create STEAM problem scenarios aligned to their content areas and draw from other disciplines without explicitly teaching those content areas. For example, in one science classroom, Ms. Becker designed a unit around investigating the text *The Ghost Map*, which is a nonfiction text about the 1854 cholera outbreak in London. She developed a STEAM problem scenario that examined the ways in which their city could be susceptible to epidemics. The students compared the densities of London (employing statistics and ratios) to their city, as well as examining how historical factors such as the Crimean War affected this outbreak. Ms. Becker did not assess the students on the facts of the Crimean War in her science class. However, the students used this content to solve the problem around epidemics. In this way, even if teachers do not teach multiple disciplines, they can approach STEAM with transdisciplinary learning.

CONCLUDING THOUGHTS ON TRANSDISCIPLINARY TEACHING

In this chapter, we offered examples from a variety of settings, grade levels, and content areas to provide context-rich examples of what STEAM looks like in practice. Transdisciplinary teaching can be a challenging strategy for teachers to incorporate. However, teachers overwhelmingly discussed its importance, as it created a platform for authentic problem solving. As one teacher described it, "I knew I was doing STEAM when the students in my class were using science, technology, social studies and so on to solve the problem. But they were doing it on their terms. It wasn't like they said, 'Oh, I am using science now,' but it is what made sense to solve the problem."

CHAPTER 5

Valuing the A in STEAM

Moving from STEM to STEAM by adding the arts to science, technology, engineering, and mathematics education can produce powerful and authentic learning opportunities (Jolly, 2014). However, in our research, we've found that simply "adding on" an arts project to a STEM unit is not enough to create these types of powerful learning opportunities. Instead, teachers need to understand the full gamut of ways to integrate arts into their teaching. To do this, we look at a continuum of art integration to give teachers ideas on how to incorporate aesthetics, design, and expression throughout their STEAM teaching.

"I understand why teachers add arts at the end of a unit . . . as an afterthought. There are ways to position arts to be a part of the problem solving, to enhance learning, instead of just an activity added in." Mrs. Harris provided this important insight during one of our debriefs after observing her teach a STEAM lesson. She is a visual arts teacher at a STEAM middle school. This public middle school houses 6th- through 8th-grade students. The students in this school identify as 48% White, 42% Black, 6% Asian, 2% Native American, 2% multiple races, and less than 2% Pacific Islander. This racial makeup is similar to the demographics of the district.

Mrs. Harris has worked with subject-area teachers for 15 years to help them see how arts enhance student learning in ELA, math, social studies, and science. Mrs. Harris had a conceptualization of STEAM that developed well before our professional development (PD) with her and her school. However, when she first started teaching at this STEAM school, she saw an opportunity to "really infuse arts into the problem solving," but she did not witness this infusion into the problem solving right away. Instead, she noted that most content-area teachers focused on art as aesthetics. While she was quick to note that this is useful, she also understands that there often missing opportunities to readily integrate arts into the STEAM problem scenarios. "Having students draw during math is using art. However, there are other ways to integrate the arts." She went on to describe one project where students created prototypes of robots. The science teacher described the arts component of STEAM as "create an aesthetically pleasing robot, which is completely fine, but if students only see art as making things pretty, we are missing an opportunity to teach them differently." Indeed, considering aesthetics is an essential skill for students to craft; however, if they only are exposed to arts as aesthetics, they may not understand the power art has in other ways, such as design, emotion, and problem solving.

THE CONTINUUM OF ARTS INTEGRATION

This idea Mrs. Harris was talking about is "arts integration"—commonly described as "teaching through the arts." Although a wide variety of conceptualizations of art exist (e.g., Burnaford, Brown, Doherty, & McLaughlin, 2007), because we work in formal education spaces, our conceptions of the arts in STEAM are different from those of educators working in informal spaces such as a museum, after-school programming, or summer camp. When we began working with schools, our goal was to create a model of arts integration that would work within the existing structures of schools such as content standards, standardized assessments, and benchmarking as well as the sometimes-rigid scheduling practices. Thus, our conception of arts is a broad view. It includes arts and humanities such as visual, English language arts, history or social studies, foreign language, media arts, and performance art. This comprehensive view of arts is necessary because schools are required to teach specific subject areas, and we want to support schools in integrating the content areas that, historically, STEM education left out. More so, we recognize the strength and diverse perspectives that these content areas bring to solving real-world problems. We position arts as an integral part of problem solving. However, we do acknowledge that there are levels of arts integration and that depending on the type of problem the students are solving, the type of arts integration should change to match the problem the students are solving. This helps to ensure the authenticity of the integration.

When we work with teachers, we focus on a continuum of arts integration. On one end of the continuum, we describe art as design, and on the other end, art as expression. An example of art as design is architects designing bridges or buildings; they are employing a specific set of skills that includes engineering principles that are related to a broad conception of arts and are therefore employing art as design. However, if those same architects consider the aesthetics of the bridge as a part of their design, they are moving along the continuum from design to expression. The architects could also consider art as exploratory if they are incorporating other components into the bridge design, such as commemorating the history of the place or exploring a new vision for the city. However, if the city that is commissioning the bridge wants to evoke a certain feeling, such as survival, and the architects design the bridge with that feeling in mind, they are employing art as expression.

Teachers find this continuum useful as they consider ways to integrate the arts into their unit planning, as the notion of an arts continuum helps them visualize different "spots along the way" from art as design to art as expression. We view the continuum as fluid, meaning that there are likely ways to include art that is not solely design or aesthetics but somewhere in between. In this way, we acknowledge the idea that the definition of art is dependent on many factors. Annette Arlander (2010) describes some of these factors when she states:

> The notion of what constitutes art (inquiry, skill, expression, originality, critical comment, decoration, entertainment, etc.) has an impact on other questions such as the role of experimentation (originality, novelty, innovation, interpretation), the characteristics of the artwork (unique object, prototype, ongoing practice, event, the artist as the artwork, etc.), the position of the artist (as auteur, producer, provider of services, first spectator, performer, etc.) and the amount of collaboration (with co-artists, spectators, participants, etc.). (p. 315)

Because of the various perspectives toward what constitutes art, it is unsurprising that STEAM adopters struggle to have a clear stance on arts integration. However, teachers have remarked that the idea of this continuum helps them understand the multiple ways to integrate art into their STEAM instruction. They often ask, "At which end of the art continuum is STEAM education?" This is such is a great question! Our answer is simple—the goal is to provide students with experiences from across the continuum because these varied experiences all benefit student learning. Therefore, we see opportunities for integrating arts from each point along the continuum.

For us, arts integration is an approach to teaching that encourages "students to construct and demonstrate understanding through an art form. Students engage in a creative process that connects an art form and another subject area and meets evolving objectives in both" (Silverstein & Layne, 2010, p. 1). Arts integration is also an opportunity to think about the way students engage in learning outside the classroom and an opportunity for using the connected learning framework in schools. One of the goals of connected learning is to foster self-expression, and when viewing arts as expression, this is an opportunity to support students in this important process.

THE VALUE OF ART IN STEAM

When schools transition from STEM to STEAM, the question of the A in STEAM becomes apparent. This is critical because without the A in STEAM, the classroom becomes a STEM classroom. As a reminder, we view STEAM as different from STEM in that it begins with a problem for students to solve, and the arts are an integral part of that problem-solving process—not just an add-on to a STEM project.

Because we view the A in STEAM as arts instead of art, we look to integrate arts in a variety of forms and ways. This broad view of art includes visual, performance (e.g., drama, music), ELA, social studies, media arts, and creative writing. We find that teachers are more comfortable with this idea of integrating multiple types of art, instead of just creative arts (e.g., visual, performance). However, teachers still gravitate toward visual arts when they are defining arts—but, interestingly, not when they begin designing the units. In fact, during our STEAM PD, the teachers become more comfortable with the other forms of art, especially the media arts, which points to the need to allow time for teachers to explore integrating different types of art. Also, we found that allowing time for teachers to brainstorm different ways to integrate arts was beneficial. We use the view of Smilan and Miraglia (2009) that art integration should be parallel to the other disciplines. This perspective helps to hold art and the other STEM disciplines on the same plane. Instead of viewing art as an "extra" or a "special" class, this equal perspective values both art and discipline concepts. For example, during a PD, a group of teachers created a problem scenario around protecting wildflowers at a local park. When they began looking for ways to integrate the arts, they considered having the students paint a still life of flowers. The teachers discussed how this felt like an "add-on," or unequal to the other disciplines. They felt it would not be part of the problem solving. Next they thought about also having the students digitally publish the paintings using Google Sites, with descriptions of the flowers and their importance in the environment. However, the still life felt like a part of the problem-solving component. We value "art for arts' sake," and as a result, we regularly encourage teachers to integrate arts beyond the problem solving.

One of the goals of STEAM is for schools to see the importance of art in the everyday world, and for solving real-world problems. Authentic art integration is one way to provide students with examples of art as a way to solve problems. Therefore, we are honoring the way authentic arts integration is defined, as learning meaningfully connecting both art content and art instruction. Additionally, authentic arts integration is a part of the problem solving, meaning that art is used to understand complex social issues (Smilan & Miraglia, 2009). These skills are indispensable for students to become literate in both critical thinking and the creative process. With this view, students can engage with real problems that involve critical thinking—and are art-based. Often, meaningfully applied art-integrated learning provides students with ways to utilize different perspectives during the problem solving.

ART AS THE BACKBONE OF PROBLEM SOLVING

When we met with Mrs. Harris to discuss ways to position arts as a component of the problem solving, we looked at a STEAM scenario and brainstormed ways this could be altered to include multiple opportunities to integrate the arts throughout all of the middle school classes. Therefore, the problem scenario was solved in all of disciplines (ELA, math, science, and technology classes). Sometimes, tweaking an existing unit is a great way to extend the inclusion of the arts beyond aesthetics. The problem scenario we began with was:

> Each year, thousands of hatchling turtles emerge from their nests along the southeast U.S. coast and enter the Atlantic Ocean. Only an estimated 1 in 1,000 to 10,000 will survive to adulthood. The natural obstacles faced by young and adult sea turtles are staggering, but increasing threats caused by humans have brought sea turtle populations very close to extinction. Today, according to federal lists, all U.S. sea turtles are endangered, except for the loggerhead, which is listed as threatened. The Greenville Zoo would like to create an educational tool that the zoo will display on World Oceans Day next to a student-created model of a sea turtle. Both the tool and the turtle will help visitors learn about sea turtles, the risks that they face, and how to help.

Real-World Problem Solving

The scenario's real-world problem occurred close to the students' homes. Many of the students saw or heard of the turtles because of the proximity of the ocean and nesting sites near our community in South Carolina. The local zoo guided our scenario. First, the zookeeper at the Greenville Zoo and our teachers met to discuss the upcoming World Oceans Day and ways in which the school and zoo could work together to create educational materials for zoo visitors. The zoo did not dictate the type of educational resources they wanted, but requested that the focus of the materials be on the challenges that sea turtles face, and concrete actions that South Carolinians can take to alleviate these challenges. The zoo requested both digital and paper materials. They also wanted a physical structure, such as the sea turtle model, to draw visitors into the zoo. The zookeeper recorded herself reading the scenario and provided information about World Oceans Day. The teachers used this 10-minute video during class to introduce the problem to students, and then the teachers asked students:

- What are your initial thoughts about the problem?
- Why do you think this problem exists?
- What are some ways to solve this problem?

After the students formed groups of three or four (according to shared interests), they researched the problem. During their research they determined the appropriate venue for presenting their findings. The students would deliver their creations to the zoo so that the zoo could use them as educational materials for the World Oceans Day event (e.g., poster, children's book, digital presentation, commercials). The next day, students were given a list of websites to begin their research, but they found other resources as well. Students shared this research with the teacher via Google Docs so the teacher could formatively assess their progress. Although students focused their research on one area of interest, all groups were required to analyze the birth and death rates of sea turtles, the historical trends of these population changes over the years, and differences among a variety of sea turtle species. Based on the results of their formative assessment, students continued to research, often with more specific direction from the teacher. The teachers required the students to research possible evidence-based reasons for changes in populations. To do this, they considered changes in turtles' food, oxygen, water, and other resource supplies.

During math class, the students predicted what would happen to sea turtle populations over time if resources continued to decrease. To do this, they looked at graphs of previous and current populations to make predictions based on these changes. In science class, they identified factors that could increase sea turtle populations, and explained how these changes in the ecosystem could cause changes for sea turtles and other organisms. For example, they looked at the temperature changes in the ocean and predicted whether the ocean waters could cool to a particular degree, and how that would change the populations. They also looked at the amount of beach that was protected to predict if protecting beaches from building was a factor that could increase sea turtle populations. In their technology class, the students created a video game where the baby sea turtle had to avoid predators to survive. When the students created the sea turtle model, they were engaged in art as design.

Art as Design

During art class, the students made the model sea turtle out of wire mesh and covered it in a newspaper. The students from all classes worked together to build one model. The wire mesh served as the base and the newspaper as the covering. The students used a papier-mâché technique involving newspaper, white glue, and water to cover the wire mesh mold of the sea turtle. At the end of the unit, students presented their research and their educational materials at the zoo. The students' presentations varied from videos of news stories about their problem of study to traditional Google Slide presentations.

Because the Greenville Zoo requested a model sea turtle for World Oceans Day, the students experienced a real-world lesson in creating a sculpture within the parameters of a deadline and a budget for supplies. The zoo did not make any specific recommendations as to what they needed; instead, they just requested a giant sea turtle model that could serve as a display. The zookeeper visited the school twice during the project. One visit was during the middle of the project to answer students' questions in a large forum; the other was during the final days of the project to see the unveiling of the sea turtle model, which was eventually brought to the zoo by zoo staff and displayed for World Oceans Day. This unit included aspects of art as design when they were building the turtle, and art as aesthetics when they were painting the sea turtle. However, Mrs. Harris saw opportunities for arts as an expression as a part of this unit.

Art as Expression

She saw an opportunity to help the students understand the different threats the sea turtles face. So she began this lesson on art as expression by having the students define movement and migration, and then list types of movement. Next, she asked students to think about a time when they moved from one location to another. She had the students write about whether they had ever "migrated" (i.e., moved to a new house). Students watched as Mrs. Harris demonstrated a "paper relief" technique, which is an art technique in which shapes are made from paper and arranged from larger to smaller sizes. First, the students created a paper relief of the sea turtle migration map, based on the content they learned in science class about where sea turtles move during their life cycle. Then students placed the migration paper reliefs on a black sheet of paper. This black background helped the colored rings to stand out. This activity highlighted the students' understanding about migration patterns and life cycles.

Then Mrs. Harris asked the students to share a time they had migrated, and students created a paper relief based on that personal experience with migration, such as moving from one city to another. The individual shapes on the reliefs reflected the feelings that students had during their personal experience with migration. Students did not merely relate their feelings; instead, they were asked to dig deeper and specify an event during which they experienced movement. Some of the students drew on their feelings about moving to middle school from elementary school, moving from one church to another, or moving from one state to another when their parents relocated for jobs.

Ultimately, students understood the idea that movement is a necessity among all species—including humans. Afterward, Mrs. Harris asked the students to reflect by completing artist statements. An artist statement is a description of what the art piece means to the artist, how the piece was made, and the rationale behind its meaning. Student statements were five to 10 sentences long and described how they could respond to emotions aesthetically and authentically. For example, Fernando, a student in the art class, described how his paper relief helped him to understand how his migration from one city to the next was an uncomfortable journey at the beginning, but now his new home feels more like home than the previous one.

Figure 5.1. Completed Sea Turtle That the Students Named "Gary"

He described making the relief in the shape of different homes, with the previous one in the distance and the new one bigger and more vibrant. In this example, the student is using art in a different way than design or aesthetics. Mrs. Harris describes this difference as "when a student uses art as an actual part of the problem solving, it changes the way they would typically solve that problem. In the sea turtles project, once the students had thought about solving the problem about arts, their ideas changed."

Student Inquiry and Expression Across Disciplines

After the unit, Mrs. Harris reflected on additional possibilities for student inquiry and expression. In a social studies class, students could examine problems of global ethics and the destruction of the environment for profit. Students might explore, "What is the responsibility of businesses to protect the Earth and what are the roles of governments and individuals?" Engineering and design classes can focus on themes such as sustainability and the invention of new green products as alternatives to non-biodegradable products. In other subjects, such as service learning, students can inquire about social activism and the role of the arts in getting messages to the public. In social studies, students can also begin to question human experiences and the migration of refugees for political, religious, and economic reasons. Regardless of the extended inquiry question, the key to making these inquiries relevant for students is to include places within these units where students can personally connect with the topic and express their creativity.

INTEGRATION OF ARTS ACROSS GRADE LEVELS

When teachers infuse the arts into their STEAM instructional plans, students engage in new and creative ways. However, the ways in which teachers infused the arts differed across the grade levels. Here, we provide grade-level examples that hone that creativity and engagement.

Early Elementary

In our work with schools, we witnessed opportunities for art as design, aesthetics, and expression, even with young learners. Young children are very creative, and it is essential that they have opportunities to express this skill. However, at times we witnessed teachers considering arts integration as crafts. While crafts certainly have a place in schools, the risk of art as only crafts (or only focused on aesthetics) is that it does not represent the multiple perspectives and viewpoints that can be brought in through different types of art. For example, in a 1st-grade classroom, students were designing windows that would discourage birds from running into them, which was a significant cause of death for certain birds in their area. The 1st-graders came up with creative designs such as bird feeders that would lure the birds away from the windows toward the feeders using music that mimicked bird calls. Other designs included incorporating more stained-glass windows, which would be less likely to confuse the birds. The students employed both design and aesthetics in their problem solving. Thinking about combining design and aesthetics in classrooms might lead to creating a paper cutout of the bird types. This bird cutout might be useful in understanding the anatomy of the bird, but the teacher would need to ensure its relevance to the problem. This added component could be showing how the anatomy of birds might make them susceptible to predators.

Upper Elementary

Fifth-grade students investigated aqueducts in a problem about how Charleston could examine ways that Europeans use aqueducts in their city planning. This research on aqueducts led them to research the Spanish artist Antoni Gaudí, whose Park Güell is well known for its stunning mosaics, but

Figure 5.2. Gaudí-Style Mosaics

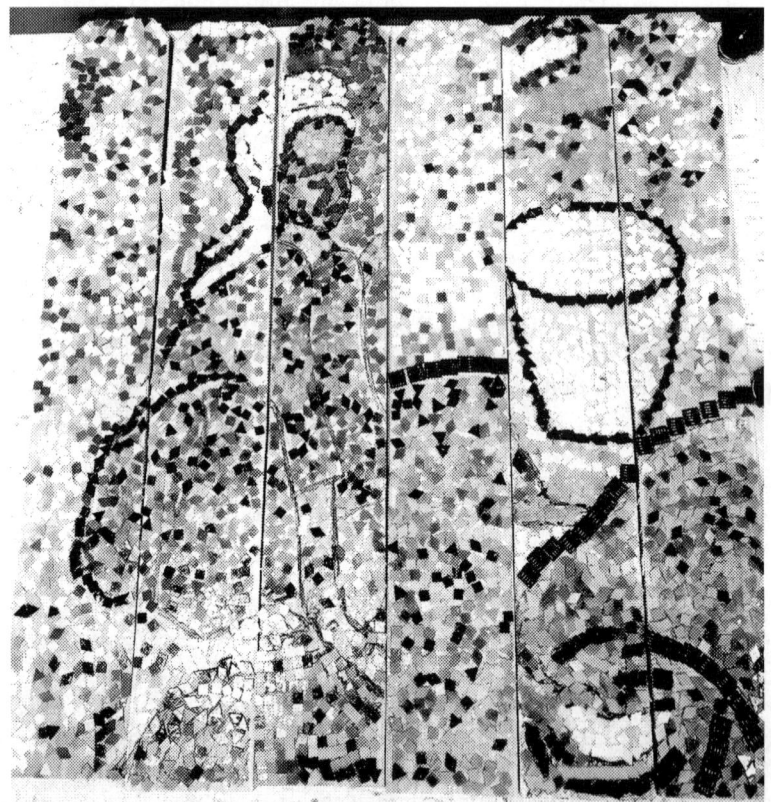

also for its construction. It was designed to ensure a way for water to flow down to the city to make sure the residents had access to the water. At the time of the park's construction, potable water was a scarce resource. The park is a nature preserve today and represents how aesthetics, design, and emotion can all be used in combination to solve a problem. The students mimicked Gaudí's mosaics but also added their creative designs to fit into the historic downtown Charleston area.

Middle School

Although the sea turtle project describes one way to integrate arts through design, aesthetics, and emotion, there are other examples of how art can be integrated, including performance art. In one middle school, the STEAM project centered on the topic of water footprints and how wasteful U.S. citizens are with our water. The students discovered that Cape Town, South Africa, was going to run out of water in the next couple of months. As a result, the students performed scenes from the musical *Urinetown*, which depicts a similar scenario in which the government begins to charge a hefty fee for the use of any water, including public toilets.

CONCLUDING THOUGHTS ON THE A IN STEAM

The A in STEAM is articulated in many ways. In our work, we found that a broad conception of arts helped teachers to provide different experiences of arts integration for students. As a result, the teachers were able to authentically integrate arts into their classroom instead of relying solely on the art teachers to be in charge of this integration. Importantly, the arts played a role in the problem solving, which provided students with opportunities for arts integration across the continuum, including art as design and art as expression. It is our hope that by providing students with these opportunities, the students will become more creative problem-solvers.

Part III

MAKING STEAM WORK

CHAPTER 6

How to Assess STEAM Learning

In this chapter we discuss one of teachers' biggest concerns—assessment. Teachers often ask us, "How do I ensure that the students will still understand the content?" This concern is an important one. Throughout this chapter, we address this concern by tackling an important element of STEAM assessment—embedded formative assessment. The second critical piece of STEAM assessment we will address is authentic summative assessment. After discussing these two components, we will talk about how to assess students when they are working together in groups. This chapter explains how to develop assessments to ensure that they are aligned to both the standards and the problem that the students are solving. Doing so involves formative and summative assessment, as well as peer and self-assessment. We also take a look at how to assess students when they are working in groups.

A DIFFERENT APPROACH TO ASSESSMENT

Ms. Hart, a 7th-grade science teacher, reflected on her initial thoughts about assessing students during STEAM teaching:

> STEAM teaching is different from my typical teaching. So it makes sense that the assessment is different. At first, I thought this would be hard. How would I assess their learning? However, I have found if you do the work of aligning the scenarios to the standards during the unit planning, and if you think about the type of things that would be done to solve the problem, it became more comfortable, and they inherently were aligned to the standards.

She pointed out that to ensure that the assessments align with the standards, teachers need to plan at the beginning phase of the unit design. Beginning with the standards is similar to the principles outlined in Wiggins and McTighe's *Understanding by Design* (2005). *Understanding by Design* asks teachers to consider the desired results or the priority learnings carefully and then create curriculum with these priority learnings in mind. The authors refer to this as backward design because often teachers design the assessments at the beginning of the curriculum design process. Beginning with the end

93

goal in mind allows teachers to create units aligned to the learning objectives. This alignment alleviates a common concern among teachers who are new to STEAM teaching.

EMBEDDED FORMATIVE ASSESSMENT

In the STEAM conceptual model, the goal is for students to participate in multiple types of inquiry processes, develop specific skills such as problem solving, and collaborate in various ways. Thus, a multiple-choice assessment represents a misalignment between the authentic, student-driven aspects of STEAM (Gulikers, Bastiaens, & Kirschner, 2004). Therefore, as we developed this conceptual model, we were careful to align the assessment practices to the type of instruction and learning expected to promote STEAM goals.

As discussed in Chapter 1, a critical component of any educational model is assessment. Because one of the instructional approaches is teacher facilitation instead of direct instruction in STEAM learning, teachers often express concern over how and when to assess students. When they implement their first STEAM unit, they often worry about whether they have assessed their students frequently enough during the unit. Ms. Hart noted this during a reflection:

> I tried to incorporate a STEAM unit at the end of the last school year. I say tried because, looking back, I feel like I could have done so much better in ALL areas but especially assessment. Next time I implement a STEAM unit, I will add in the formative assessments during the planning process. I think this will be more beneficial to my students and me in checking their learning progression. Without this planning, I did not adequately formatively assess during the implemented STEAM unit. I recognized this when the students were presenting their final projects. I realized how I needed to support them along the way better.

Ms. Hart reflected on her struggles with including formative assessments throughout the units. We call these types of assessments "embedded formative assessment," as the term *embedded* indicates that teachers insert assessments during the planning process. As teachers are sketching out their unit plans, we recommend that they think about checkpoints, or points where they check in with their students about what they have learned. When teachers think about embedding formative assessment during the planning process, it becomes a part of the daily lesson plan, and it is more likely to become a part of the implementation.

In STEAM teaching, we focus on planning out the formative assessment strategies during unit planning. However, we are not suggesting that all formative assessment should be preplanned. We believe there are many opportunities for impromptu formative assessment, such as classroom discussions or one-on-one conversations with students. We encourage these organic conversations, which regularly lead to valuable information about students' content knowledge. Since students might be at different stages of the problem-solving process (e.g., some might be finishing up brainstorming ideas, others might be researching, while others might be collecting data) during STEAM instruction, it is crucial that there are also structured opportunities for teachers to check in with students to see where they are in the process of STEAM learning.

These embedded formative assessments can take many forms:

- short two- to four-question quizzes: online or paper form of a quiz to address specific content knowledge.
- think/pair/share discussions: students are given time to first "think" alone, then "pair" up and share ideas together as a pair, and then "share" with the whole class.
- draft thinking presentations: short, 2-minute, in-progress presentations where students share where they are in the process and what they need help with.
- check-ins: teachers create points in the progress where students must check in with them and receive feedback on their ideas or project.
- prototyping a model: students create a prototype of their model and receive feedback on it prior to creating the final model.
- exit tickets: students are asked a question about the class to reflect on, typically on a 3-by-5-inch notecard, and hand it to the teacher on the way out the door as their "exit ticket."
- self-reflection: teachers ask students a series of questions that ask them to reflect on their content knowledge.
- 1-minute papers: students respond to a prompt in 1 minute, which gives teachers input about the students' knowledge of the topic.
- observation: teachers can observe small-group sessions to determine how students are understanding the topics with their peers.

Ms. League, a 7th-grade science teacher, created a formative assessment to assess her students' knowledge of issues jellyfish are facing.

The STEAM problem scenario she created was about jellyfish and potential ways to help these creatures. It read:

If you spent any time at the beach this summer, you probably noticed the large amount of jellyfish washed up on the sand and swimming around in the shallow water. There appears to be more and more jellyfish making their way into our waters at Myrtle Beach, and with jellyfish come jellyfish stings. In August, Myrtle Beach lifeguards reported treating up to 100 jellyfish stings per day! When this occurs, the National Weather Service issues Beach Hazard Warnings, keeping swimmers out of the water and giving tourists a reason to travel somewhere else. Why are we experiencing a jellyfish invasion? To claim that Myrtle Beach is under "attack" by jellyfish, you need data to support it. Working with the Myrtle Beach Ocean Rescue and the Coastal Carolina University Marine Biology department, compose a population report for jellyfish on our coastline. With your team, research jellyfish and their preferred living environment. Are human actions impacting the ocean water and making jellyfish migrate to our coastline? Develop a diagnosis of the jellyfish problem in Myrtle Beach and brainstorm solutions. Compose a plan for a potential solution you think would be beneficial to implement in Horry County. Include a budget to present with your solution. This department runs the beach renourishment program and is responsible for construction and drainage systems throughout the county. Want to take on a different role? Perhaps an environmentalist? Animal rights activist? Your presentation should involve a plan of action regarding jellyfish, but doesn't necessarily need to "get rid" of them. Create a PSA to inform beachgoers of the hazards of jellyfish and how best to ease the burn of a jellyfish sting. This will accompany a jellyfish display your team creates for the Myrtle Beach Welcome Center.

She created her formative assessment in the form of tweets, which asked students to concisely and creatively craft their responses. To do so, she gave the students the following prompt: "Even though your group is still in the process of making your proposal to present to the Engineering Department of Horry County regarding the jellyfish, the tourists are getting restless! The head of social media for the City of Myrtle Beach is allowing you to send out three tweets: (1) Diagnosing what you believe to be the cause of the jellyfish. (2) Short description of how you came to this diagnosis. (3) Brief overview of a potential solution. "By asking students to create tweets, she connected the assessment task to the problem-solving scenario because tweeting is a way information is shared with the public."

During the formative assessment, the goal is twofold: to understand what the students know, and to provide students with an opportunity to understand their knowledge. The first goal is a goal that teachers readily understand—formative assessment tells teachers about what the students know. It helps to inform their teaching to see if the teaching plan needs to be altered to meet the students' needs. The second goal provides students with insight into their learning process. This insight is vital to provide students with an understanding of how they learn and can support them throughout their career (Black et al., 2004).

Technology Use with Formative Assessment

Teachers regularly utilize technology for formative assessment (Beatty & Gerace, 2009). Technology can be a great way to reduce grading time and provide students with immediate feedback. For example, Google Forms, Socrative, or Kahoot! are examples of tools teachers can use for formative assessment. While each of these tools is different, they all essentially are ways for teachers to create online quizzes. Ms. Hart noted that technology aided her during the STEAM units in several ways:

> I use Kahoot! and Plickers because they are so effective. The kids love them. I particularly like that Plickers provides an easy way for me to assess them while only using technology on my end. Socrative and Exit-Ticket also work well in my classroom. I love the idea of assessing students through games, and Socrative provides that option. I use exit tickets almost daily in my classroom, so a digital format of that would fit well into my classroom. The most significant advantage of using technology for formative assessment is teachers can see the results immediately, which is beneficial for on-the-fly assessments. I can see right away where students are confused and I have the ability to address it right away. Another advantage is students are exposed to many different apps, tools, and websites, which can help increase their literacy with technology. Students can also be assessed in a way that doesn't feel like an assessment. My students requested to play Kahoot! after ending a lesson early one day. I love that students wanted to participate in an assessment!

Here, technology assisted her in providing a pathway for assessment—and the bonus was that the students enjoyed using the technology. As with all technology, teachers need to make sure it is the right fit for their school and students. Some tools are geared toward a variety of ages (e.g., Kahoot!), but others might only be appropriate for older students because of the limited ability to add images and the focus on the written text (e.g., Google Forms, which does not have a built-in audio component). Instead of encouraging one type of technology tool over another, we suggest that teachers test out a variety of tools to see what best fits their classroom needs. By using a variety of technologies, teachers can ensure that they are connecting with the way students are learning outside the classroom; this is a component of connected learning framework, as new media amplifies the opportunities for connected learning. Specifically, by tapping into a variety of technologies, teachers can ensure that students are staying up-to-date with technological advances.

The Frequency of Formative Assessment

When teachers begin embedding formative assessments into their unit plans, they often ask about the frequency of formative assessments, wondering,

"How much is enough?" While this is a tricky question to answer, we understand the need for guidance. Typically, we look to the number of standards the unit will address. For example, in Ms. Hart's classroom, the STEAM problem scenario she created was:

> Just eight days ago there was an earthquake of a 2.0 magnitude in Cityview! In fact, earthquakes happen all the time and are becoming more and more prevalent. While most are minor, and we cannot even feel the Earth shifting, significant earthquakes cause severe damage and have the potential to harm and kill people. Your task is to determine whether or not a significant earthquake could ever take place in Cityview. Your team will gather your evidence to support and defend your answer to this question. To communicate this information to the public, you must create an informational brochure or video expressing your claim.

> **Driving question:** Could a significant earthquake take place in Cityview? Explain why a significant earthquake could take place in Cityview.

In this STEAM problem scenario, Ms. Hart's 7th-grade students worked to solve a real-world issue about the likelihood of a major earthquake in their town. Ms. Hart aligned this scenario to the following NGSS standards:

- Develop a model to describe the cycling of Earth's materials and the flow of energy that drives this process.
- Construct an explanation based on evidence for how geoscience processes have changed Earth's surface at the varying time and spatial scales.
- Analyze and interpret data on the distribution of fossils and rocks, continental shapes, and sea floor structures to provide evidence of the past plate motions.
- Analyze and interpret data on natural hazards to forecast future catastrophic events and inform the development of technologies to mitigate their effects.

This unit addressed four student performance objectives, which teachers should assess during the summative assessment. However, as we review these standards, it is essential to know if the students understood the content behind the process skills before the summative assessment. Therefore, we recommended that Ms. Hart embed four formative assessment tasks into her unit. These assessment tasks could take on a variety of forms but, again, must connect to the standards. For example, the first standard asks students to develop a model describing the cycling of Earth's materials and the flow of energy that drives this process. Therefore, we suggested designing an embedded formative assessment to understand if the students understand how the Earth's materials (water, rock, etc.) move and how energy is involved in that process.

For the second standard, it is important to assess students on the geoscience processes on the Earth's surface area. Then students need to be able to construct explanations based on evidence. Breaking the standards up into parts helps teachers assess students in smaller, more manageable areas of learning before assessing them on the full standard. By aligning the formative assessments to the standards, teachers can ensure that the STEAM units align to the standards, and the formative assessment provides teachers with an opportunity to assess their students before the summative assessment.

When teachers embed the assessments throughout the learning process, they provide frequent and high-quality feedback to the student. Therefore, embedded assessments serve to enhance student learning either by bridging the gap between a student's current understanding of content and the learning objectives. It helps to prevent the challenges Ms. Hart experienced in her first STEAM unit. She remarked:

> Because I had not assessed the students along the way, it was not until I looked at the final projects that I realized the students did not fully understand how energy is involved in the geological changes. Had I planned for those assessments during the unit design, I would have prepared for that. During a STEAM unit, it is important to know that learning specific content knowledge does not get lost amid all of the other real-world, authentic, relevant, collaborative activities that are going on. A quick formative assessment can highlight which students may not have mastered some specific math/science/language arts skill. These short assessments are especially useful because they make it clear whether everyone understands what he or she needs to do, so we can move on. Or if no one understands adequately, then I would need to plan something to reteach the entire class, or a few students don't understand, in which case, I can target specific students for reteaching without taking time away from the whole class.

Here, Ms. Hart reflected on the multiple ways formative assessment could have been used in her classroom. As we mentioned previously, the lack of planned formative assessments is often an issue the first time a teacher implements a STEAM unit. However, we cannot underscore enough the importance of using formative assessment strategies in STEAM.

STEAM units are interdisciplinary, so it is imperative for their success to make sure that the students are at a level of understanding for each discipline. Data reporting as part of a formative assessment will be useful, mainly when covering disciplines where the teacher may not be an expert; the teacher can take these data to the expert teacher during collaboration.

These data will let the teacher know what the students are misunderstanding and will help guide the STEAM teacher in planning follow-up lessons.

AUTHENTIC SUMMATIVE ASSESSMENTS

Aligned with the STEAM conceptual model, authentic tasks are a vital part of what students do during STEAM learning. The goal of these tasks is to mimic what is happening in the real world. Therefore, the way teachers assess students should line up with the way the teachers teach during STEAM lessons. We call these summative assessments "authentic assessments."

In authentic assessments, students are asked to apply the knowledge and skills they learned during the STEAM unit but also mirror what would be done to solve the problem. We define authentic assessment alignment as being a connected problem the students are answering. For example, in the earthquake unit, the students gathered existing data from the National Oceanic and Atmospheric Administration (NOAA) about the occurrence of earthquakes in the area. Next, the students created models based on the evidence they gathered on NOAA's site. They used this information to create educational materials to help prepare the community in the event of an earthquake.

Ms. Hart graded the students formatively during the data collection and interpretation phases, and summatively during the modeling and presentation of the educational materials. The models and educational materials represent authentic assessments because they mimic what geological experts do when they are conducting a risk assessment. If we compare this to a multiple-choice test that asks students to calculate percentages based on data presented, the former represents a larger project that involves more discipline integration. The latter (multiple-choice test) assesses students' knowledge of the standards and is considered a valid assessment. However, the models and educational materials provide students with an opportunity to apply their knowledge of data interpretation in a real-world context. As Ms. Hart described, "When I saw the models the students created based on the data gathered, they represented something you would see if you were watching a news story on earthquakes. They were real!"

Table 6.1 provides an example of a rubric of a summative assessment that a 4th-grade teacher, Ms. Fields, created. The STEAM scenario, which was based on a real situation, was to create an inclusive play structure:

> You were recently at Ashley Dearing Park and noticed a child sitting on the bench not playing. When they tried to play, the equipment proved to be too dangerous for them because they had cerebral palsy (CP). This made you think about how the playground and surrounding landscaping could be modified to better suit all kids, including kids with special needs. Decide on a piece of playground equipment that can be modified

Table 6.1 Example Rubric for Authentic Assessment

Criteria	4	2	0	Points Assigned	Feedback
Scale Drawing	Blueprint shows the footprint of the design and layout. Has an accurate and consistent scale.	Some errors on the scale drawing or scale is not applied consistently.	No attempt to draw a true scale drawing.		
Scale Model	Scale model accurately reflects the CAD design. Has an accurate design and consistent scale.	Scale model and CAD design do not match and/or the scale is not applied consistently.	No attempt to create a scale model.		
CAD Design	CAD design has accurate measurement and reflects both the scale drawing and scale model.	CAD design is missing accurate measurements and/or does not reflect the scale model/drawing.	No attempt to create a CAD design.		
Consistent Scale	Scale is consistent among the blueprint, scale model, and CAD model.	A few discrepancies in the scale appear but do not affect the overall design.	No attempt to maintain a consistent scale between the models.		
Neatness/ Overall design	The design is well-thought-out, meets the requirements described, and is obviously backed up by research. Each representation is completed neatly.	The design is thrown together and does not meet all requirements.	No attempt to meet the project requirements or create neat models.		
			Total Score		

it is also critically important for girls and students of color, who often say that they do not get an opportunity to demonstrate success in school. Studies point to whole-classroom discussions and standardized testing as favoring boys and white students more often (Morris, 2007). Therefore, by offering other ways to assess student knowledge, authentic assessments can create a pathway for more equitable participation in school.

Despite successes, our teachers regularly described the challenges they face when implementing authentic summative assessments. Specifically, district-mandated assessments can create a roadblock to authentically created STEAM assessments. Mr. Andrews described his experience during a reflection: "In my district, they give teachers assessments to use, usually traditional assessments, we are expected to use during teaching. Those are nonnegotiable. However, I try to incorporate alternative assessments as much as I can. Which is far less than I would like. However, it is usually formative versus summative." We encountered many experiences like Mr. Andrews's. While there is usually not an option to disregard the district-mandated assessments, we find that when teachers align the authentic assessments directly to the standards and evidence this alignment in the rubrics, school districts are more willing to allow the authentic assessments. It is essential for teachers to communicate with their district leaders about how authentic assessments are a valid measure of the standards.

Importantly, although we describe authentic and embedded assessments, we want to be careful not to limit the types of evaluations teachers can design. There are many ways teachers can assess student knowledge, including models, stories, performances, scripts, and designs, among others. The goal is that assessments reflect the learning objectives and content standards of the unit.

PEER AND SELF-ASSESSMENT IN STEAM

In the previous two sections, we outlined two types of assessment in STEAM: formative and summative assessments. In both of these assessment types, teachers can build in experiences for the assessments themselves to be a learning experience. The authentic summative assessments can be an opportunity for students to learn new skills as they produce a wide variety of products, projects, and tools. However, through the use of peer and self-assessment, teachers can turn assessments into rich learning opportunities.

Peer Assessments in STEAM

Through peer assessments, the learning opportunities are bidirectional, meaning that both the assessor and the assessed (the student) learn through the process. If we look to the earthquake example, Ms. Hart could have structured the summative assessment to include peer assessment as the students were creating educational materials. We recommend that this peer assessment come during the draft phase of the project so the students have time to utilize the feedback and make changes to their project. If teachers wait until the end of the unit, the feedback, while valuable, often is not incorporated.

Giving students opportunities to learn how and when to incorporate feedback is an essential skill. Also, when teachers implement peer review during the draft phase, assessors often learn from critiquing others' work and often incorporate those ideas into their own work. At times teachers are concerned that this is copying; however, if we think about how all the projects should look different in STEAM units, this is rarely an issue. Instead, think about when you have noticed an excellent idea, such as a way to organize kitchen or closet spaces. You could incorporate that idea into your home, but the materials you use and the way you organize would be slightly different.

During the peer review process it is vital for teachers to provide students with specific guidance on how to give feedback. For example, if Ms. Hart used peer review when the students created their educational materials, she could have created a list of prompts for students to consider, such as:

- Does the text provide enough information about the likelihood of an earthquake in the area? If so, explain how. If not, suggest improving it.
- Does the text include accurate facts and figures about how likely an earthquake is? If so, explain how. If not, suggest improving it.
- Are the visuals easy to read and make sense given the topic? If so, explain how. If not, suggest improving it.
- Think of a suggestion about the visual organization of the educational material that would enhance its readability.

This type of specificity helps to avoid comments such as "Good job!" or "Looks great!" and instead provides targeted feedback for the peer on how to improve. It is also helpful to model this activity before the first peer assessment. Specificity helps to ensure that the feedback is constructive but not unkind. Often phrases such as "Consider . . ." or "Perhaps . . . " soften the language and set the tone for helpful feedback.

Another way teachers can provide opportunities for peer review is through the use of rubrics. Many authentic assessments include a rubric to guide the students toward expectations. Teachers can use these rubrics to guide the peer review process. Students primarily evaluate their peer's work using the existing rubric to provide guided feedback. When teachers use this strategy, they often comment on how the process benefits both the reviewer and the student receiving the feedback. For example, one student noted, "I realized I forgot to do a part of the project when I was reviewing their work. I went back to my project and added in the missing piece."

For STEAM teachers, peer review can be built into the authentic assessment seamlessly, as these assessments are multifaceted, which creates an opportunity for feedback because there is not just one correct answer. The feedback will look different depending on the problem the students are solving as well as the experience of the student providing the feedback. In this way, the feedback will be specific and unique each time.

Self-Assessments in STEAM

Similar to peer assessment, self-assessment is a useful strategy providing students with an opportunity for self-reflection on their learning process. This self-reflection is a type of metacognition, or how we know what we know. As the students progress through learning experiences such as STEAM, which asks them to draw on multiple knowledge types such as movie production, song creation, scientific explanations, or poems, providing them with time to self-evaluate can help them understand how they are learning during these experiences.

It also can provide students with insights into how they can improve; however, similar to peer assessments, we recommend providing students with specific guidance to aid this process. By giving the students guidance, they can learn the process of reflecting on their learning with support. Over time, students begin to reflect on their learning on their own. This self-reflection is a skill that students hone over time with STEAM education.

STEAM ASSESSMENTS ACROSS GRADE LEVELS

Assessment should look different across the grade levels, and STEAM assessment is no different. In this section, we provide examples of how teachers in early elementary, upper elementary, and middle school can think about how to vary assessments for their students.

Early Elementary

In early elementary, where there is a wide variety of literacy skills, using visuals during assessment is often helpful. However, some STEAM teachers report that there are ways to integrate technology with formative assessment. Ms. Birch, a 2nd-grade teacher, described her experience with one type of technology tool:

> Kahoot! is one I have been using in the classroom that my students and I love. It is age-appropriate for 1st grade, and you can use it with any

topic. Also, Socrative is a useful tool for my classroom. I like that it gives you real-time feedback, as well as percentages. It has a feature that will read questions to students. That is important to me, since almost all of my students are developing readers. I want the formative assessments to reflect their knowledge of something, not their reading ability (unless I am assessing their reading skills).

Upper Elementary

For upper elementary teachers, being able to create an authentic assessment that assesses students' knowledge across a variety of subject areas is incredibly useful. Not only does it save time during grading, but it provides students with opportunities to be creative and demonstrate their abilities in new ways. Mr. Folly, a 5th-grade teacher, noted that in a project about an invasive beetle that was harming baby birds in the local area, he was able to design an authentic assessment aligned to math, science, engineering, technology, and ELA. The students created a trap for the beetles, which required the use of math skills such as scale and proportions. They were also using their engineering design skills to build the traps.

As a part of the process, they researched the life cycles of the beetles and predicted ways to interrupt this cycle. Also, they constructed explanations for how this invasive species got out of control. Last, they created digital stories tracking the changes in the birds' habitat due to the influx of the beetle. Mr. Folly designed a rubric that included all of the subject areas and incorporated peer review during the unit. He described his experience with this authentic assessment: "I was amazed at the ways I was able to assess the students according to a wide variety of standards. Once I had aligned the STEAM unit with the standards, constructed the assessment, and flushed out the rubric, it all fell into place."

Middle School

For middle school teachers who teach 80–125 students each day, providing feedback to students through formative assessment can be a considerable challenge, as STEAM teachers have remarked. Ms. Hart noted, "I have to know what my students think so I can support them. Knowing what my students are thinking is even more important during STEAM when the students are involved in different projects and are at different stages of the process." She went on to describe how, at times, technology aided her in the formative assessment process and how at other times it makes more sense to use low-tech options:

I think the advantage to using technology for formative assessment is both the immediate feedback it can give and data reporting/collection/

sorting. In teaching, time is precious, so having an app or website that can give you the data without you having to do anything is enormous. It saves me time, and I do not have to keep track of any papers. I teach middle school, and even when students are thoroughly proficient with their devices and the apps we are using, we still manage to lose time (someone forgot to charge it at home and can't find a charger, someone cannot connect to the Internet, etc.). It just isn't as reliable as physical assessments. But you do save much time grading and providing feedback thanks to these apps, so it is a give-and-take. Some days, I cannot handle 30 kids telling me their computers will not work, so we do it on paper. Some days, I want to play Kahoot! and get a data report to see where they are in the STEAM process.

Here, Ms. Hart described the give-and-take that most teachers face with technology. However, the end goal remained the same with formative assessment: Teachers understand what their students have learned and are able to provide feedback to the students.

CONCLUDING THOUGHTS ON STEAM ASSESSMENT

STEAM teaching presents an opportunity not only for a different type of classroom environment that promotes real-world problem solving, but also an opportunity for assessments aligned to these environments. By embedding the assessments throughout the learning as well as creating assessments that represent the type of work that would be done in the real world to solve the problem, teachers provide students with authentic experiences from the beginning to the end of the unit.

CHAPTER 7

STEAM Across
Different School Settings

In this book, we provide a conceptual model for teachers and schools to implement STEAM in their classrooms. Still, as teachers think about transitioning to STEAM, we often get questions that are context-specific. For example, teachers ask, "What if my school is not a STEAM school?" or "What if my teaching team does not implement STEAM?" or "How can a whole school become a STEAM school?" These are all important questions and suggest one thing: Context matters. Every school is different, with different students filling each classroom. In the previous chapters, we included examples from across different grade levels (K–8), content areas, and school settings.

In this chapter, we address the particulars of three common contexts when implementing STEAM: a new, whole-school initiative; a traditional school where several teachers are implementing STEAM; and an existing school that is reorganizing to become a STEAM school. More specifically, the three contexts we examine are (1) Franklin Middle School, a new school that was structurally and curricularly designed for STEAM learning. Franklin Middle School is an urban school with a racially diverse student population that is 52% White, 32% Black, 9% Latino, 2% multiple races, 2% Asian, and less than 1% American Indian or Pacific Islander. The school is 42% female and 58% male. It is a public school with an attendance zone and an option to apply to the school as a part of the district's school choice program. (2) Stafford Middle School, a traditional school without a particular focus on STEAM curricula. It is also an urban school, with students identifying as 38% White, 30% Black, 18% Latino, 11% multiple races, 2% Asian, and less than 1% American Indian or Pacific Islander. The school is 51% male and 49% female. The school is a public school with an attendance zone. (3) Washington Middle School, an existing elementary school that recently adopted a STEAM approach to teaching and revamped existing curriculum to match this learning approach. It is a rural school (transitioning to suburban with the development of the town) and its students identify as 48% white, 35% black, 11% Latino, 5% multiple races, 1% Asian, and less than 1% American Indian or Pacific Islander. The school is 46% male and 54% female. The school is a public school with an attendance zone. In each of these settings, teachers were new to implementing STEAM. However, each of the teachers experienced different levels of support and as a result achieved varying levels of success. As a reminder, all of the schools are real schools; however, we use pseudonyms to protect their identities.

This chapter provides administrators, instructional coaches, and teacher educators with ways to think about supporting teachers, but also to help teachers think about work-arounds as they begin to implement STEAM in their classroom. Therefore, we provide a description of the STEAM problem scenario as well as a snapshot of a specific lesson. We also provide reflections from a teacher in each setting, offering a firsthand experience of what it is like to implement STEAM for the first time in these situations.

CONTEXT ONE: A NEW STEAM SCHOOL

At Franklin Middle School, teachers work in learning pods, or central physical meeting spaces that promote interdisciplinary collaboration. The school uses common planning time built into the weekly calendar, and each student receives a touchscreen computer for academic work. Instructional leaders encourage co-designed curricular units. For example, you might see science, social studies, English/language arts, and math teachers working together to present students with an integrated unit on designing an ecosystem and proposing a plan to accommodate a new animal habitat at the local zoo. The unit might involve designing and presenting a plan for an ecosystem considered an appropriate habitat for the species, space and budgetary considerations, sustainability, and historical significance to the local area—drawing on all of the above mentioned disciplines.

The STEAM Problem Scenario

The lesson began with Ms. Craft, a 6th-grade teacher, showing students an electronic book on the Promethean board, and reminding them to complete an assignment that involved watching a short presentation and taking a quiz within a digital textbook on their laptops. Students were given 10 minutes to play a digital board game with their group on classifying animals, followed by watching a 5-minute video on vertebrates and invertebrates. Ms. Craft reminded students about videoconferencing with a local zookeeper and an upcoming virtual zoo field trip before posing the problem they were to collaboratively solve:

> The zoo needs your help! The zoo has noticed that many people do not know the difference between a vertebrate and invertebrate. Because part of the zoo's mission is to educate the community, they want to be sure visitors understand this difference. The zookeeper is asking our

class to help our local zoo by creating a relevant fact sheet and media to educate the public on vertebrates and invertebrates. Zoo media relations needs your expertise in presenting visitors with this information.

Ms. Craft discussed more specific requirements and distributed a criteria sheet on Google Classroom outlining potential Internet research and images or use of plastic animal figurines for their research and media presentation. Students began working in groups of three to choose specific animals for their research. Ms. Craft circulated, reminding them what they needed to do to complete their research, while students openly chatted about their tasks and, at times, asked Ms. Craft for assistance with information, clarification, or to preview their presentation designs. On this particular day, students were searching the Internet and designing with paper and pencil, flip charts, and video and presentation software.

Ms. Craft's Reflections on STEAM Teaching

In all, Ms. Craft implemented three extensive STEAM units during the first year of her work at Franklin Middle School. She reflected on her successes and challenges and provided advice to other teachers considering STEAM teaching. She talked about integrating both new and old pedagogical practices in her teaching, altering what was effective in the past to offer STEAM learning experiences. This instructional change included more attention to student choice and focused efforts to get students to collaborate. She explained:

> I jumped in feet-first and students started by designing their native plant garden based on the school's yard design. I found that giving students a variety of choices and using Google Classroom and all of the related apps have increased collaboration. In some of my STEAM units, students were presented with a problem and had to find a way that was best to present their idea or topic to the rest of the class. They could even choose drama, speech, or songs. Dramatic role-play has been fun to use in the classroom, and it has been helpful to see if students understand the context and meaning of, say, science vocabulary. I have also tried to develop stronger units with a focus on careers and jobs and connecting them with recent events.

She further commented on incorporating methods she had effectively used in the past:

> Some teaching methods that I have used for years continue to be very effective. I check their science notebooks for reflections and understanding of the day's lesson, and I also continue to use rubrics as a means

of grading projects. I also use peer review for student accountability. I probably do that more now, but I have been using peer review for a long time.

Ms. Craft reflected on the challenges she encountered as she changed her teaching approach:

> Even with block scheduling, I feel some time constraints when trying to team with other teachers. At times parents are concerned about projects with collaborative work, wondering if grades represent the team or their son/daughter. Although our students have access to much technology, I wanted them to make an iMovie, and we had limited iPads. I had to consider training them to use the platform, since some students are not used to movie editing. However, I think iMovie is the best to use for quick, simple, and user-friendly movie making. Students who would not typically want to complete an assignment or work willingly with a partner loved showing their creativity by making a movie, even if it was not their favorite topic.

When reflecting on her overall practice, Ms. Craft's most significant concerns involved appropriate use of technology, promoting inquiry skills in students versus providing them with too much information, and covering the requisite content to meet 6th-grade science standards.

CONTEXT TWO: A TRADITIONAL MIDDLE SCHOOL

Second, we present the case of Ms. Hart, a 7th-grade science and social studies teacher at Stafford Middle School. Ms. Hart has been teaching for 6 years, although this is only her second year in this district. Stafford Middle School is a traditional middle school in that there is not a particular focus on STEAM curricula. Instead, three teachers from this school attended the summer STEAM professional development (PD), and they implemented STEAM in their classes. While they have one another for support, Stafford Middle School has not adopted STEAM as a schoolwide initiative. Ms. Hart's case provides context for teachers who are interested in implementing STEAM practices but may not have a full commitment (e.g., scheduling restraints, lack of schoolwide STEAM adoption, inflexible pacing) from their school.

The STEAM Problem Scenario

As mentioned in Chapter 6, Ms. Hart designed the following problem scenario:

The community has stated that it would like bridges that can withstand weather but also that are aesthetically pleasing. In order to do this, you need to understand current weather patterns and traffic flow/changes, as well as any restrictions (these could be environmental, government regulations, or economic).

Then, to simulate one activity that students might do within the STEAM unit, the community were instructed to:

- Divide into groups of 5–6 people.
- Create a paper bridge that spans 1 meter and will hold a water bottle for 90 seconds using only the materials provided (paper, scissors, and tape).
- Draw your plans and record your data on the Data Recording Sheets provided at each station.
- Complete this task in 15 minutes or less. . . . Ready? Set . . . Go!

After the activity was completed, a brief discussion ensued that helped community members understand how the scenario was connected to the activity, and how other activities might be aligned with each of the STEAM disciplines.

A question-and-answer session and follow-up survey to elicit feedback regarding the effectiveness of the workshop can also assist schools in developing their strategic plan well before the STEAM school opens or new curriculum is presented to students. It provides an opportunity to solicit volunteers to serve as mentors and experts in STEAM units, and the survey can help improve and direct the next community visioning day.

Resource Assessment

Assessing resources means that school- and district-level resources are appraised, documented, and distributed to teachers to understand what is and is not possible when planning STEAM units.

Technology integration is the backbone of many STEAM units, yet many schools begin STEAM instruction with little thought toward additional access to Internet sites or devices. In some cases, teachers and students are unaware of subscriptions or access to district-adopted digital tools. While it may not be possible to anticipate all technology needs before STEAM units are created, at minimum policies and a plan to provide increased access and identify the logistics should be in place. STEAM instruction can be effective with low-tech options; however, no-tech options undercut significant means for students to collaborate; innovate; communicate with mentors, peers, and teachers; and share with the broader community. Technology integration will and should look very different for young children (e.g., more app-based

Just eight days ago there was an earthquake of a 2.0 magnitude in Cityview! In fact, earthquakes happen all the time and are becoming more and more prevalent. While most are minor, and we cannot even feel the Earth shifting, significant earthquakes cause severe damage and have the potential to harm and kill people. Your task is to determine whether or not a significant earthquake could ever take place in Cityview. Your team will gather your evidence to support and defend your answer to this question. To communicate this information to the public, you must create an informational brochure or video expressing your claim.

In this lesson, students worked in teams to research fault lines located in the state, and learned the reasons why earthquakes happen. Some groups also spent time researching where significant earthquakes occurred and the implications of these devastating events.

Ms. Hart's Reflection on STEAM Teaching

Ms. Hart's approach to STEAM often included a real-world problem that the students would solve, but instead of including all the disciplines, it often included only two or three. This problem scenario foregrounded the STEAM unit, and incorporated science and technology readily, but Ms. Hart also integrated other disciplines at times as well. Below Ms. Hart describes how she integrated math into her science lesson about earthquakes:

This week, I was able to integrate math with science: a bit of a cross-disciplinary integration. The lab we did was entitled "Voyage to the Center of the Earth," and the requirement was for students to make a model of Earth's layers on a piece of ticker tape. The students used scaled measurements of the Earth's layers and measured out these layers on ticker tape.

Ms. Hart's context was different from Ms. Craft's in that she was one of three teachers from her school who had participated in any STEAM professional development. However, because she worked with a different team of teachers to plan units, she attempted to train her teaching partners (other science and social studies teachers) in STEAM. To make STEAM manageable, she commented:

This week in science I began planning for my team's first full-blown problem-based unit. I designed this unit to be a shorter, more manageable unit in order to help myself, my team, and my students get acclimated to this kind of instruction. It appears, from the first six weeks of class, that our students are not accustomed to group work or independent learning, and so this project is a good step and likely to benefit them.

The next week, a STEAM-related activity that the students participated in was the creation of a topographic map model. Students were given Play-Doh and were instructed to create their mountain made of concentric layers. They were to draw the profile of the mountain and then take the mountain apart to trace each layer, creating a topographic map. They were instructed to include a river and a steep and sloped side of the mountain; other than that, they could make their mountain look however they wanted. We noted that while this was an excellent engineering and science activity, it was divorced from any real-world connection. To make this a STEAM activity, she might challenge students to develop a mountain that serves a particular purpose, or design a model topographic map of a specific region in the state that needs a particular map for a specific purpose.

CONTEXT THREE: AN EXISTING SCHOOL TRANSITIONING TO STEAM

The third case illustrates the practice of Ms. Walls, an instructional coach at Washington Elementary School. Ms. Walls was a teacher for 10 years before becoming an instructional coach last year when Washington Elementary School became the first official school in the district to adopt a STEAM approach. Before shifting toward STEAM practices, the teachers underwent districtwide PD wherein they collaboratively planned a STEAM unit across multiple disciplines (i.e., science, technology, engineering, arts and humanities, and mathematics). These planning sessions occurred during the school day, and the district hired substitutes to allow teachers to plan the unit together. The following year, they began implementing this planned unit.

The difference between this school and the first one is that the school was not created with STEAM in mind, like Franklin Middle School. Still, teachers received supports such as common planning time and opportunities to change the schedule so that students could have longer blocks of time to work on the STEAM projects.

The STEAM Problem Scenario

Washington Elementary School's entire 3rd-grade teaching team planned a STEAM unit wherein the students were learning about food deserts and were asked to figure out what could help local food banks provide fresh fruits and vegetables to people who do not have access to these foods. The students decided to build a school garden. As a part of this project, they planned, created, and built an outdoor garden. The goal was to grow vegetables that could be donated to a local food bank. The project included designing a garden with multiple raised beds, compost bins, and an irrigation system, as well as a crop rotation schedule. To design the plans, the students created 3D models of the garden using Google Draw. Then they presented the plans to a panel of experts, with one plan selected by a panel. After the panel chose the plan, the students implemented it by creating schedules for the classes and preparing and planting all of the beds. Once the students harvested the vegetables, they donated them to a local food bank. The teachers divided specific tasks into their subject areas. For example, in ELA they worked on the presentations for the panel. In science class, they learned about the appropriate plants for the climate region and the life cycle of plants. In math, they calculated the surface area and volume of the spaces and created materials lists based on these measurements.

Ms. Walls's Reflection on STEAM Teaching

As described above, the common planning time provided opportunities to integrate the content in a variety of disciplines. Ms. Walls discusses this in her reflection when she states:

> Our whole 3rd-grade team met to work on our STEAM unit, and everyone is on board with our plan to have students create proposals to fix up the outdoor classroom. Our social studies teachers came up with a better way to connect the unit to their content: they are going to have some groups come up with a better plan for irrigation in the garden and connect these ideas of irrigation to the ways in which historically farmers in the state had to work around issues of drought and flooding. These common planning times help to make sure the larger STEAM project is being connected in each of the subject areas.

Another strategy Washington Elementary School employed was altering the schedule so students and teachers would have longer blocks of time to work on the project. Below is Ms. Walls's statement about the structure of these alternative scheduled days:

> I took the Google survey results from a few weeks ago and placed the kids into a group based on their interest. The classrooms will be working on classifying and caring for the plants currently in the garden. During social studies time, we will work on a plan for irrigation, math classes are trying to improve the pathways and gathering areas, and science classes are coming up with plans for the raised beds. We had the students go to their homeroom classrooms for a 1st–2nd period and then return for the 5th–6th period; that way they have large chunks of time to work on the project. We plan to use this alternative schedule for 5 days total.

While not required to implement STEAM, this scheduling flexibility provided students with opportunities to delve deeper into the content and begin to problem-solve ways to build the school garden and work in their collaborative groups for extended periods of time. It recognizes that learning should move beyond a discrete set of content or skills and that when given longer chunks of time to work on projects, content and skills can be applied in authentic ways, such as in the example above to create a school garden. Additionally, this flexibility allows for experts in the community to work with students, providing a real-world context to STEAM projects. Ms. Walls discusses ways in which they involved experts in the field to help students draw deeper connections about the project:

> We introduced the project with a PowerPoint that showed pictures of the garden's current state, the project goals, and the driving question, "How can we make Falcon Falls a true outdoor classroom for Washington Elementary?" Mrs. Anderson, a retired teacher who originally started the outdoor classroom, spoke to our kids about the history and creation of the garden. We also had a horticulture expert come in and talk to the kids. He gave them tons of useful information. The kids were even more excited about their projects after he left because he gave them so much more information to add. It was amazing to watch how excited the kids were about this project and hear them say at the end of the day, "I love school!"

These experts inform the curricula in multiple ways. In addition to providing real-world connections, they also help the teachers see the importance of STEAM teaching. Ms. Walls describes this in her reflection:

> One of the unique parts of my job is that I get to meet with members of the community and share our STEAM experiences. We have a STEAM Advisory Committee that meets just about every month. This group is members of the business community who come to find out what we are doing and how they can work with us. We keep hearing over and over how the processes and skills that we are teaching students through STEAM are what employers need.

THE KEY TO STEAM IMPLEMENTATION: REMIXING EDUCATION

Next, we discuss the three instances of teachers implementing STEAM teaching in their classrooms, drawing on different contexts to highlight what each might imply for teacher preparation, professional development, and classrooms wishing to integrate STEAM teaching. An underlying constant among the instances is the idea that a STEAM teaching approach was not an add-on to the curriculum, a new curriculum, a specialized program, or an entirely new pedagogical approach. Instead, the teachers "remixed" education to alter, appropriate, or shift existing curricula and pedagogy to enact new (STEAM) teaching with varying levels of success.

A School Built for STEAM Teaching and Learning

Ms. Craft's case demonstrated that even with the structural (learning pods, schedule, movable furniture) and pedagogical support of a STEAM-created school, the teacher found it helpful to rely on tools, resources, current curricula, and prior effective teaching strategies. For example, while Ms. Craft stressed new instructional approaches such as problem-based learning, student choice, and collaborative work in the STEAM units, she typically began with direct instruction. She used the Promethean board and encouraged student responses by having them interact individually with digital quizzes or responding as a whole class to short video clips. Her instructional units included topics she had explored numerous times during her 12 years of teaching and, similar to prior approaches, she rotated from group to group while students worked collaboratively. Ms. Craft's use of science notebooks, rubrics, and peer review may have looked slightly different from traditional teaching regarding content and expectations, but they were a clear alteration of already existing approaches. She also used many of the same digital tools she had been incorporating in student learning for a few years.

STEAM Teaching in a Traditional School

Like Ms. Craft, Ms. Hart used problem scenarios to engage her students. Although her teaching tenure was relatively short—just 6 years, so she was arguably less entrenched in the "craft of teaching," she still relied on past practice to guide her instruction. Her earthquake unit and topographic map activity were not a marked departure from previous topics addressed in her curricula, and she found cross-disciplinary approaches (math and science or science and engineering) relatively easy to enact. That said, she made shifts toward STEAM in her teaching practice. For example, she was able to create real-world problem scenarios to guide her teaching. Additionally, she discussed the importance of formative assessments during the STEAM units and discussed how technology aided in being able to do this quickly and adjust her teaching based on this information.

Instructional Approaches in a STEAM-Themed School

Ms. Walls's teaching context was unique in that she served as a support for other teachers in the school, and she had administrative and schoolwide support to assist in STEAM implementations. The additional flexibility to alter current schedules, disrupt pacing, and modify current units of study allowed her to assist in bridging many disciplines. The creation of a sustainable food garden was a transdisciplinary unit that addressed and involved numerous disciplines naturally through the nature of the problem, which was providing a sustainable food source. Ms. Walls's teaching teams were intimately involved in the planning of the unit and creation of an engaging problem, but they focused primarily on supporting learning by modifying what they already had expertise in. In essence, the teachers remixed content and strategies they were comfortable with to support the larger unit. This remixing was evident in the involvement of all the teachers at the school. For example, during the garden project, the health teacher connected the project to her teaching, and the teachers connected ELA to the problem by using debate as a way to help the students understand the complexity of food deserts. The art teacher was also involved in that students created murals for the gardens that depicted the strength of the community. In this way, the students were able to experience connections beyond one classroom. The teachers felt that this was one way the disciplinary lines could be blurred so that students were able to experience authentic problem solving.

SUPPORTING STEAM ACROSS GRADE LEVELS

Early Elementary

When looking at the three scenarios, early elementary teachers often begin with STEAM by looking at their thematic units. Beginning with a thematic unit was apparent regardless of whether they were designing STEAM units in a brand-new STEAM school or a traditional school. While this is often a natural first step, we found that early educators had the most success when they remixed this thematic unit, such as a pumpkin unit, into a problem. Consider, for example, "The farmers at our local pumpkin patch are in trouble. Most of their pumpkins are not growing, and they need your help to find out why!" While the students could still learn all about pumpkins, and even visit a pumpkin patch, they are solving an age-appropriate, standards-based problem where they can investigate how plants grow.

Upper Elementary

Even though upper elementary teachers taught a variety of STEAM topics and units within different contexts, they all changed the learning environment to afford students' collaborative work. Additionally, all found some degree of success whether the learning environment was built for STEAM or modified for collaborative work. This is one area where upper elementary teachers regularly find success. Because upper elementary teachers often have their students for longer times during the day than middle school teachers, there is an opportunity to teach the necessary skills of collaboration. Upper elementary teachers often point out that the task must be worthy of group work, which means that each person has a specific task to do that cannot be completed alone. Additionally, they discuss the importance of teaching the students to rely on one another to solve the problem instead of coming to the teacher for help. The teachers note that this latter issue means they are relinquishing control to the students, but if the STEAM problem is designed to encourage real-world problem solving and divided into manageable tasks, shifting the control to the students becomes more natural.

Middle School

One challenge for all teachers is pacing. However, for middle school teachers, when they are working across different content areas within a teaching team, this can present a unique challenge. Ms. Craft and Ms. Walls found ways to alter their planning and pacing schedules in contexts that demonstrated varying levels of support. Whether implementing shorter units, STEAM activities with one or two teaching partners, or schoolwide units, the teachers believed that flexibility in planning and pacing was paramount to success in altering their practices. While the first case showcased a school built with STEAM in mind, in the other cases the teacher was able to adjust planning and pacing within their more traditional contexts. Addressing challenges to planning and pacing by providing context-specific solutions during school meetings, on-site professional development, and preservice teacher education courses may assist in overcoming barriers to implementation and challenges before beginning STEAM units.

CONCLUDING THOUGHTS ON
STEAM IMPLEMENTATION IN DIFFERENT SCHOOL SETTINGS

To shift teaching practices and embrace STEAM methods effectively, the teacher might draw on and alter or remix existing practices instead of adopting entirely new curricula, specialized programs, or engaging in entirely new pedagogical practices. The cases above illuminate how STEAM teaching can be implemented with some success whether the context is a school built for STEAM teaching, a traditional setting, or schoolwide STEAM-themed activities. The cases acknowledge that there are some challenges no matter what the context.

Finally, we recognize that conceptualizing STEAM as remixing education is not entirely novel. Many innovations stand on the shoulders of prior effective practices and learning environments; however, viewing STEAM through this lens whereby teachers implement STEAM practices to "suit their style" (Jenkins, 2008), and providing reliable evidence of its effectiveness, may offer educators a starting point to step into STEAM no matter their context.

CHAPTER 8

Challenges to STEAM Instruction

This chapter details instructional challenges faced by STEAM teachers who developed and implemented STEAM units in their classrooms using the STEAM conceptual model. We provide excerpts from reflective journals that teachers kept during their STEAM teaching highlighting the significant challenges noted by the majority of teachers, which included challenges related to planning, pacing, discipline integration, and student understanding. We then discuss potential solutions to overcome the challenges, noting that all of the solutions should begin with administrative support.

Below, Mr. Thomas describes his initial challenges with STEAM during his first attempt at implementing STEAM in his science class:

How can I teach all of STEAM in a science class, and still stay on the pacing guide? For the zoo project, I left too much math out. I wanted them to determine the cost of building the exhibit, daily feeding cost, any extra employees if needed, transportation for the animal, and to determine if the zoo needed to raise admission due to the new exhibit.

Mr. Thomas was not alone in his struggle when he wrote about implementation challenges with STEAM instruction in his 6th-grade classroom. He kept a reflective journal to document his STEAM journey over the course of a semester. He, along with dozens of other teachers, wrote at least one journal entry per week while actively implementing their STEAM units. They also wrote some additional entries as they prepared for the STEAM unit implementations, and afterward as they reflected on what went well and what they hoped to improve upon in the next unit.

Another 7th-grade science teacher, Ms. Murray, commented similarly in her journal, believing that this new way of teaching initially took more time, throwing off her pacing, as did the need to meet standards at specific times of the school year. These issues sometimes made STEAM units challenging to implement. She stated:

This week I was able to find a little more balance between giving the students freedom to learn and guiding them to the concepts I need them to learn for the standards. I did not give them notes as I have done in previous years. Instead, we read a newsletter that was written explicitly for the 7th-grade science standards. They watched a digital slide show and then discussed the content and worked with partners to make a classification chart using Google Docs to help direct their plant garden designs. I felt that overall it went much better because they were in charge of their learning, but it takes more time for their group work and I am afraid I will fall behind in covering all of the science content.

THE NATURE OF CHALLENGES WITH STEAM EDUCATION

As part of our longitudinal study regarding STEAM teaching practices, we investigated the challenges faced by teachers when implementing STEAM instructional practices in their classrooms (Herro, Quigley, & Cian, 2018). We asked teachers to keep journal entries to help us determine patterns in instructional challenges. Some of the challenges they wrote about were directly related to STEAM instruction, and others were similar to challenges faced by STEM educators, such as additional preparation time, access to resources, learning new content, and effective assessment (Laboy-Rush, 2011). In our early research to understand and potentially avoid some of the same issues, we also looked at STEM instructional issues, as STEAM was novel. We noted that STEM implementation challenges often center on conceptualization issues—where educators and stakeholders (e.g., community members, parents, administrators) are not clear about what is, and is not, considered STEM teaching or learning activities. Unsurprisingly, teachers using our STEAM conceptual model rarely struggled to conceptualize STEAM (Herro & Quigley, 2016), which is likely due to the emphasis on developing a shared understanding through the model to create STEAM units. In STEM education, conversely, there is also a lack of understanding and expertise regarding discipline integration, as well as inadequate leadership to help educators navigate the complexity of changing instructional models (Portz, 2015). These same issues were readily apparent in the teachers we worked with who were integrating STEAM units.

Shifts in Teaching and Challenges in STEAM Instruction

In our work, we found that teachers overwhelmingly believed that STEAM instruction shifted their teaching to be more problem-based, student-focused, and collaborative, which included a multi- or transdisciplinary approach. This instructional shift, for many teachers, came with some challenges, as STEAM naturally involves more people, different resources, increased collaborative work by teachers and students, and a new way of thinking about disciplinary teaching.

Challenges Related to Planning

Planning posed a challenge for teachers implementing STEAM units in two different ways. First, teachers discussed the challenges they faced when planning STEAM activities aligned with standards and the content they were required to teach. Second, many of them talked about the difficulties in planning a project with their colleagues who were either less interested in or less informed about STEAM education. (Lack of interest by colleagues was rarely an issue if they had attended the STEAM PD.) These two challenges go hand-in-hand. For instance, the teachers discussed challenges they faced when planning units while keeping standards and discipline alignment in mind. They often pointed out that if they were able to plan with interested content experts in their school (e.g., a science teacher collaborating with math and art specialists, or a math teacher working with social studies, science, and music teachers), the STEAM unit posed fewer challenges in discipline integration or transdisciplinary teaching. Ms. Rice articulated this challenge when she told us:

> Sometimes it seems that the nature of the standard dictates the ease with which teachers implement STEAM units. This week is a case in point. The standards we covered involved "seeing" and "hearing" in relation to the structure of the eye and ear and correlation with waves and wave behaviors. Simply put, the essential questions we need to answer are, "How does hearing and seeing take place?" Regarding planning, these standards do not readily lend themselves to being drawn out and made into a STEAM unit. I might be able to do this better if I had a team to plan with, but it is hard to get other teachers to participate because they do not understand that STEAM can be used for so many ideas and projects. It is tough to get people to work with me if they have not had STEAM training.

Pacing Issues: Time Management, Policies, and Assessment

At some point in their STEAM unit implementations, most of the teachers we worked with expressed concerns over the expected curriculum pacing of required units of study, and the amount of time required to adequately implement their STEAM unit when integrating existing standards and curriculum into the unit. They believed it took longer than they anticipated to carry out the daily activities and shift their instruction. This was due, in part, to providing less direct instruction and increasing time to facilitate more student-led learning and project work. This increase in instructional time was particularly noticeable to them the first time they taught a STEAM unit, and less apparent when they implemented subsequent STEAM units or refined and retaught the same unit for the second time.

They noted that without careful planning, the STEAM units sometimes prevented them from covering other concepts required during the semester. The teachers felt pressured to prepare for tests; compress projects when the schools shortened teachers' instructional time due to breaks in the school calendar or inclement weather; or move on to other, non-STEAM instructional units. A few teachers discussed the developmental level of some of the students, English language learners, or students receiving special education services as taking more time than anticipated to comprehend STEAM concepts fully, although teachers did not see this as markedly different from what they face daily in terms of differentiating instruction. Many teachers acknowledged that shifting their instructional role from direct instruction to facilitation was time-consuming. Ms. Bryant summed this all up when she said:

> Time is the biggest impediment for me. We must take into account lost instructional time due to club meetings, testing dates, snow days, and school assemblies. We are also hindered by the amount of material we must cover in the short amount of time provided. My students enjoy the project- and problem-based lessons, and I hope with time that I will be able to incorporate these activities more efficiently. I am still familiarizing myself with the flow of the 6th-grade curriculum, so I hope to improve my time management in the years to come.

Mandated policies related to assessment, and occasionally access to resources, were also challenges to STEAM instruction that teachers had to creatively work around. For example, district curriculum guides in many schools dictated skills and standards that should be addressed during particular times of the calendar year, and teachers felt pressure to adhere to the content and time periods strictly. They also recognized the impact of mandated testing, associating the amount of time spent on testing and interruptions in the calendar as interfering with extended blocks of time to efficiently implement project-based activities.

One of the teachers, Ms. Powers, was frank when discussing the impact of policy issues toward curriculum expectations and assessment interfering with STEAM instruction in their classrooms:

> I'm always concerned about the time and pace of not interfering with what I am required to cover. This unit, according to our district curriculum guide, should have been completed in December. I'm just now in the early stages of this unit. So the pressure to complete the unit promptly impedes me. This week has been a real challenge. Our class schedules were utterly turned upside-down for two days because of required MAP testing, and for two others we had students in and out of class for MAP makeup testing. We spent much time getting students

back into the regular class routine. We learned that the funding that had been approved by the district for the butterfly garden portion of this project is not happening, so we are considering a GoFundMe page, as the kids have been working so hard on this project.

Alternative assessments are often used to measure learning in many constructivist and project-based learning environments (Anderson, 1998), and thus are an excellent way to evaluate STEAM learning. In Chapter 6, we discussed embedded formative assessments and authentic assessments as two ways to alternatively assess learning in STEAM instruction. Assessing project work, discussions, and noncognitive skills can be challenging if ample time and support are not given to develop, implement, and revise the assessments. In our experience, with adequate professional development (PD) to assist in building appropriate assessments aligned with STEAM instruction (see Chapter 6), most teachers are very supportive of developing and implementing nontraditional assessments. However, one clear challenge in using these assessments is district policies, typically mandated at the state level, that require traditional standardized tests. For STEAM instruction this often poses challenges related to time spent creating and implementing two assessments, as well as garnering legitimacy from parents and community members who believe that state- and district-sanctioned assessment policies take precedence over alternative assessments (Haney, Lumpe, & Czerniak, 2003). As one teacher, Mr. Banks, noted, "I have to give district-created tests. I formatively assess students and grade project work along the way, but I don't have a choice about the tests."

Discipline Integration Challenges

Discipline integration in STEAM instruction can be especially challenging for teachers who are content experts in one subject area and are often required to cover particular content tightly aligned to disciplinary standards. Because of this, it is easy to fall prey to favoring a primary area of expertise when developing a STEAM scenario and unit. As a reminder, teachers should purposefully write the scenarios to foreground locally relevant problems. Ostensibly, most real-world problems are transdisciplinary and can address a variety of standards. However, writing a transdisciplinary problem does not ensure that teachers have the expertise to address all disciplines within the unit adequately. This level of expertise can be particularly true for upper-grade levels, where the STEAM problems increase in complexity. For example, consider the difficulty for teachers in creating authentic problems with engineering as part of the lesson design without engineering curricula, training, or prior experience in project-based learning or STEAM instruction. One 5th-grade science teacher, Ms. Amend, wrote about her frustration with discipline integration in her reflective journal, saying:

My animal unit is turning out to include less math than I would like, but I am integrating science, technology—and trying to integrate engineering. My teaching partner, Corrine, is doing something completely different so when we finish, we can compare the two. She seems to understand how to integrate math better than me, so I feel like mine is on the not-so-good side as the students are using basic math facts. The students have been collaborating with Google Apps and learning from each other, but I wish I had taken the time to develop the discipline integration with other teachers and maybe experts at the zoo. I am also all thrown off because my entire scope and sequence are out of order from how I usually teach this.

In our STEAM research, we were somewhat surprised to learn that teachers we worked with identified difficulty in integrating math content and standards within authentic scenarios more often than any other discipline, whether or not their primary area of specialization was in math. Some even expressed concerns over whether experts who were enlisted to talk with their students about real-world issues understood how math might be used as something other than for a skill-based application with a somewhat disconnected focus on the problem. For instance, one math teacher, Mrs. Vasquez, noted:

There is always a lot of art integration in these lessons. Science and technology are also used a lot. Math is usually the weakest area in the STEAM process. The main subject that I teach is math. I know it's always hardest for the other teachers to connect the math. Guest speakers we have [to assist in connecting STEAM learning to the real world] can never relate to math teachers. They always do some simple thing that we cannot use. It is sad for me because I love math.

Student Understanding

A significant challenge to STEAM instruction is ensuring that students understand the concepts within the problem posed in the STEAM scenario and that they can develop, master, and apply all the underlying skills and processes within each STEAM activity.

Students may have difficulty with a self-directed inquiry or collaborating with peers when problem solving, as many are accustomed to heavy reliance on their teachers and traditional ways of learning (Radziwill, Benton, & Moellers, 2015). In some cases, students do not understand the content presented or explored without a great deal of reteaching, differentiated instruction, or time to practice. Varying developmental levels, second-language learners, and students with learning or other disabilities require the same level or increased levels of support (depending on the activity) that they do in classrooms with direct instruction, but frequently teachers assume that students' engagement and project work completed with peers demonstrates an adequate understanding of underlying processes and skills. In fact, they might need other accommodations typically seen in inclusion classrooms such as increased instructional time, some small-group reteaching, and occasional individualized work (Kilanowski-Press, Foote, & Rinaldo, 2010). This challenge also points to the need for well-developed formative assessments aligned with the standards and skills in the STEAM unit. In our early work, we quickly discovered that many teachers got to the midpoint or end of the STEAM unit without a clear idea of what individual students understood or if they needed additional practice.

This challenge is demonstrated by what Ms. Simpson, a 7th-grade math teacher, wrote in her journal about a portion of a STEAM unit requiring students to change fractions to decimals:

> Even though I had grouped them with at least one strong math student, many were not able to correctly complete the processes during the group time. After allowing them to struggle for a short time (not too long, as I didn't want to lose their attention), I pulled the groups back to the class and guided them through each process. I was surprised that very few students remembered the processes even after going over them. Many in this class seem to struggle with any process that involves multiple steps and analyzing information. I think it is hard for them to direct their learning.

SOLUTIONS FOR STEAM INSTRUCTIONAL CHALLENGES

After discussing several challenges to the STEAM instruction, we focus our attention on offering potential solutions for these STEAM implementation issues. We begin by addressing administrative support, as it is the crux of any successful, scalable, innovative teaching approach (Marks & Printy, 2003).

We also include suggestions for "where to look" as a starting point for technology resources in this section. Although challenges with technology were infrequently noted in our research, we believe that finding and assessing technology resources and considering how to use them when developing STEAM units assists educators in planning for technology integration.

The Importance of Administrative Support

The challenges above suggest a distinct need for administrative support from the outset of visioning and planning for STEAM instruction. Planning allows schools and teachers pathways to success as challenges are avoided or, in time, overcome. As with any new instructional initiative, administrative support at the district (superintendents, directors of instruction, curriculum coordinators, etc.) and site level (principals, assistant principals, etc.) is crucial to addressing the challenges and offering flexibility for planning, pacing, additional time, and supportive policies. Administrative backing is also essential to offer needed resources (e.g., instructional coaches, release time for teachers to observe or work with one another, or individual education supports) to mitigate discipline integration concerns and students' lack of understanding of the content or process in STEAM. A communicated commitment to STEAM instruction (further detailed in Chapter 2) with supports that are specifically outlined by the administration team should direct district and school-level STEAM initiatives. We discuss these additional supports, which all begin with administrative decisions and resource allocation, as potential solutions to STEAM instructional challenges in no particular order below.

Ongoing professional development. One way to offset challenges before they occur is to offer intensive STEAM instructional PD and follow-up support that allows all teachers to conceptualize a model of instruction, and then reflect upon and refine their teaching practices (e.g., a model such as our STEAM conceptual model delineating STEAM practices and detailing what STEAM is and is not). While school districts vary in how and when PD is offered, most plan for PD as they implement new instructional practices. Allowing for common planning time and professional learning community (PLC) formation is a great way to get teachers on board and benefit them in planning units that extend project-based learning or multidisciplinary teaching to transdisciplinary teaching. Chapter 3 details ways to create and use PLCs in support of STEAM initiatives.

Assessment support. Understanding that transdisciplinary learning calls for formative and authentic assessments helps teachers accurately gauge student learning in STEAM activities. At the same time, teachers are required to meet content-specific standards, and STEAM units must address their content and standards or they will continue to be an add-on, extra-curricular, or elective course. Similar to the ongoing PD mentioned above, embedding PD and support where instructional coaches or PLCs assist in developing formative and alternative summative assessments while creating STEAM units and during their implementation is a way to ensure that the assessments accurately measure the learning goals. Whenever possible, offering flexibility in the types and frequency of tests that are not mandated will allow teachers time to develop and accurately assess STEAM learning. Targeted workshops to lead these efforts throughout the school year provide time and support for teachers to refine their assessments.

Collaborative planning. Focusing collaborative planning efforts across disciplines and with experts and mentors from the broader community to support the transdisciplinary nature of STEAM teaching can significantly strengthen STEAM curricula. Expecting teachers to create and implement STEAM units without disciplinary experts presents enormous challenges that they could avoid by considering collaborative teams from the outset of a STEAM unit. For example, classroom teachers might form teams by partnering with an art, music, or theater teacher and community expert (topic-dependent), or perhaps math, science, English language arts, and social studies teachers might work with a computer resource teacher and outside experts. There are many ways to construct teams that will increase disciplinary teaching and learning, including tapping into teachers or experts online. We have seen this done successfully even in smaller or rural school communities with fewer teachers or limited local access to expertise.

Adjusting schedules. Administrative support to adjust teachers' and students' daily schedules before STEAM teaching alleviates some planning issues. If possible, consider block scheduling during portions of each STEAM unit to allow for extended problem-solving time. Scheduling that offers focused, uninterrupted time for STEAM instruction is one way to solve the problems of limited time to plan with colleagues or short blocks of STEAM instructional times. There are a variety of ways to adjust planning and learning times. We have seen schools successfully implement STEAM units using 1 day a week as a "STEAM day," or by adjusting daily schedules for 3 or 4 weeks of each semester to accommodate STEAM instruction.

Supports for all learners. Carefully considering supports for struggling or reluctant learners in inquiry-based, analytical, and multistep learning processes from the outset of STEAM unit planning and implementation alleviates some of the challenges of students understanding the content or process. Teachers can proactively review the required skills and content knowledge within the STEAM unit, assess individual students' strengths and weaknesses, and develop a tentative plan to assist them. Providing coaching, co-teaching, and computer-based or volunteer supports from the outset of the unit can help ensure success for all learners.

Increased attention to technology availability and access. Before beginning STEAM instruction, it is helpful to engage in careful planning with technical support, instructional technology coaches, or library/media specialists. It is essential to keep in mind that technology should be in the hands of students, versus using it solely for instruction. That said, STEAM units do not have to include all high-tech options, nor offer individual access. Sharing devices, tools, and access is the reality in many schools, and fortunately, the collaborative nature of STEAM learning makes this less of a challenge.

Taking stock of available resources, online subscriptions, shared devices, and real technology tools (e.g., robots, circuits, e-textiles, Lego kits, coding games), with realistic expectations for STEAM activities in light of each classroom's access to digital tools, helps to alleviate logistical concerns at the outset of the unit. With a wealth of online tools such as Google applications, mobile apps, infographics, blogging sites, and presentation and visual software, there are many choices. However, as STEAM units cover a variety of topic areas and potential activities, there are no particular tools that must be used. Instead, paying attention to technology integration and digital tool use on sites such as Edutopia (https://www.edutopia.org/) or International Society for Technology in Education (ISTE; https://www.iste.org/) resources, or Common Sense Media (https://www.commonsense.org/education/), are great places to start building your STEAM repository of technology integration ideas and resources.

For young children, skill- and content-specific apps, digital storytelling, websites that offer elementary-friendly videos and games, basic drawing and modeling tools, and tangible technologies such as coding games, simple robot and building kits, or circuitry are technologies worth considering. For late elementary and middle school students, collaborative apps such as G-Suite for Education (https://edu.google.com/k-12-solutions/g-suite/), Adobe Spark videos or pages (https://spark.adobe.com/), and digital design, drawing, and modeling tools are a good fit with many STEAM units. More sophisticated robots, Lego building and programming kits, circuitry and e-textiles, and 3-D printers, which often are in makerspaces, can be easily integrated with many STEAM activities centered on design, building, or exploration while problem solving.

CONCLUDING THOUGHTS ON CHALLENGES IN STEAM

New instructional approaches are often fraught with challenges as invested educators struggle to innovate in somewhat inflexible environments (Shaffer, 2006). While STEAM instruction may suffer from some of the same instructional challenges as project-based learning, STEM teaching, and other constructivist approaches, administrative support and careful planning ahead can assure success in classrooms. Using the STEAM conceptual model presented in this book and considering ways to support teachers and students through ongoing PD, collaborative planning, individualized instructional assistance, and scheduling flexibility may significantly lessen the challenges.

The Future of STEAM

A New Beginning for Educators?

An Educator's Guide to STEAM offers a starting point for schools of education, K–12 teachers and administrators, and researchers to conceptualize and consider what effective STEAM instruction looks like in practice. It also provides the building blocks to create relevant STEAM units for K–8 students in a variety of educational settings, and then to assess the effectiveness of student learning formatively and authentically. By discussing common challenges and suggesting ways to overcome them, we have helped ensure success across educational contexts—whether you work in a rural, suburban, or urban setting, or work with elementary or middle school students.

REVISITING STEAM VERSUS STEM

The addition of the "A" to previous models of STEM education is significant. It means so much more than simply adding "the arts" to existing science, technology, engineering, and math units or activities. The "A" component indicates that as educators we are committed to taking a more humanitarian and equitable approach to learning by considering the social and creative aspects of problem solving. After all, most intractable problems are not relegated to the fields of science, math, engineering, or technology. And most solutions for wicked[1] problems (Rittel & Webber, 1974) need the innovative and creative perspectives that are present in STEAM instruction. Teachers can use STEAM to guide students to find ways to tap into the true nature of transdisciplinary problem solving through the arts and social sciences.

RECOGNIZING THE NECESSITY OF STEAM

We wrote this book because we believe that STEAM instruction is a powerful approach to teaching and learning. STEAM is a way to engage all students, but notably reengage girls and students of color, who are historically

---

1. A wicked problem is one for which each attempt to create a solution changes the understanding of the problem. Wicked problems cannot be solved in a traditional step-by-step fashion, because the problem definition evolves as new possible solutions are considered and/or implemented.

and continually underrepresented in the STEM field. The strategies outlined in this book have decades of research documenting their effectiveness for girls and students of color. These include collaborative problem solving, relevant problem-based instruction, technology integration, authentic discipline integration, and multiple ways to demonstrate knowledge. And while none of these strategies singularly is novel, the way we combine and use STEAM problem scenarios as a platform is transformative for students who feel distanced from STEM.

We wrote this book for all educators, but focus particular attention on what teachers might do, as STEAM instruction will likely originate in their classrooms. STEAM instruction can positively shift instruction and learning to mirror how problems present themselves and are solved in the real world. Ms. Harris said it best when she stated:

> I have found the joy in teaching again. Prior to shifting my teaching to STEAM, I was actually considering leaving the teaching field. I had taught for 16 years and felt that it was time to do something different. I just didn't love teaching like I used to. But after the STEAM PD and the opportunity to work with my colleagues on STEAM units, I am so glad that I didn't. The feedback from the students has been great. They are so excited about the opportunity to redesign the cafeteria [their STEAM problem is based around the problem of unhealthy food, congestion in the cafeteria, high amount of waste (including food and trash), and lack of aesthetics in the room]. Each day they come in with new ideas and questions. Their excitement is infectious and makes me love teaching again.

What is exciting to us, as researchers and educators, is that Ms. Harris is one of many teachers to share this sentiment. While STEAM teaching is not easy at the beginning, we noticed time and time again teachers persisting through the challenges. The reason for this persistence is simple: the students. Every teacher we worked with who attempted a STEAM unit tells us the same thing: The students love this type of learning. Student engagement is very high. STEAM learning makes sense to students. What we are asking teachers to do is to give STEAM teaching a chance. We believe that they will see the same results the teachers in this book describe.

MOVING FORWARD WITH STEAM EDUCATION

Using the STEAM conceptual model, described in Chapter 1, to create the conditions for STEAM instruction is an effective way to begin developing STEAM curriculum and experiences for students. Connected learning principles offer a starting point to develop interest-based, peer-supported, academically oriented, production-centered, openly networked opportunities with a shared purpose for all learners. It is a way to consider how to draw on students' diverse backgrounds and interests and to allow them to demonstrate their learning in ways they enjoy. This might be through students creating with digital media; making or building objects with wood, Legos, or fabric; expressing themselves through art or music; collaborating with one another; or sharing their work in technology-enabled environments.

Technology and innovation will continue to shift instruction and likely present new problems to solve. Schooling will not look the same in the decades ahead, which means that teacher education programs and educational research will be vastly different. Both the conceptual model we've developed and the theory of connected learning offer significant ways to improve STEAM education, but they, too, will likely change with the times. There is so much more that teacher educators, administrators, teachers, instructional coaches, and researchers can do to support STEAM education and embrace these inevitable shifts in technology and instruction. Thus, we end by offering our readers some ways to get started with a STEAM initiative or continue moving forward with STEAM education. We specifically address teachers, teacher educators, administrators, instructional coaches, and researchers.

For Teachers

Consider ways to partner with other teachers who have a common interest in innovative teaching and value project-based learning, technology integration, and authentic problem solving. Use the STEAM conceptual model and scenario-writing as a way to begin developing STEAM units. Start small, with shorter units, and spend time setting up classroom conditions that will support STEAM problem solving, including building a strong community with students' family members and experts who can assist in making the teaching approach and related activities a reality. Approach STEAM teaching as an opportunity to enhance good instruction for students.

For Teacher Educators

The STEAM conceptual model, connected learning theory, and sample problem scenarios and unit template in Chapter 3 of this book (see Figure 3.1) offer a great starting point to revamp coursework to include STEAM exercises and activities. STEAM concepts can be integrated in a manner that assists preservice teachers in creating their own standards-aligned STEAM scenarios for the developmental age that they hope to teach. The next generation of teachers might begin their careers with a solid concept of STEAM instruction for all students, and an attitude of being a lifelong learner.

For Administrators

Supporting teachers and the entire school community is key to moving STEAM initiatives forward. After developing a solid understanding of STEAM, administrators can assist teachers by making STEAM instruction a school goal, staying abreast of PD opportunities, and building a school community where innovation is rewarded. This visioning and support cannot be overlooked for successful, scalable, and sustainable STEAM programs. Recognizing that STEAM instruction will change with the times to address new problems, include new teaching staff and resources, and adapt to new technological innovations will help guide the schools' goals and PD plans.

For Instructional Coaches

Advocating for time, resources, and collaborative planning for STEAM instruction while remaining a supportive colleague will help STEAM programs flourish. Assisting with co-teaching, modeling, connecting teachers to community members and resources, sharing exemplar STEAM units, and focusing on ways to collaboratively revise STEAM activities in keeping with changing curricular goals are significant ways forward for STEAM.

For Researchers

Adopting a transdisciplinary approach to research is one way to transcend siloed ideas about how particular disciplines must be taught, studied, and shared with the broader educational research community. Connected learning theory may be a worthwhile perspective to theorize the work you do. While not easy, research across disciplinary boundaries where social scientists, computer scientists, engineers, those in the arts and humanities, and science and technology experts work together to ask questions and conduct educational research allows STEAM research to move beyond the narrow perspectives that are often found within disciplinary-focused fields.

FINAL THOUGHTS

As with many innovative teaching approaches, there is always a looming concern that the pendulum will swing and old methods and approaches will replace progress made toward new initiatives. To those who worry about whether this grand undertaking of STEAM instruction is worthwhile, we offer that any transformation that aligns with how work is really done, problems are really solved, and solutions are really found—while engaging and exciting students and their teachers—is well worth the effort.

References

Ahn, J., Subramaniam, M., Bonsignore, E., Pellicone, A., Waugh, A., & Yip, J. (2014). "I want to be a game designer or scientist": Connected learning and developing identities with urban, African-American youth. In *Proceedings of the Eleventh International Conference of the Learning Sciences (ICLS 2014)* (pp. 657–664). College Park, MD.

An, Y. J., & Reigeluth, C. (2011). Creating technology-enhanced, learner-centered classrooms: K–12 teachers' beliefs, perceptions, barriers, and support needs. *Journal of Digital Learning in Teacher Education, 28*(2), 54–62.

Anderson, R. S. (1998). Why talk about different ways to grade? The shift from traditional assessment to alternative assessment. *New Directions for Teaching and Learning, 74*, 5–16.

Arlander, A. (2010). Characteristics of visual and performing arts. In M. Biggs and H. Karlsson (Eds.), *The Routledge companion to research in the arts* (pp. 315–332). New York, NY: Routledge.

Barron, B., & Darling-Hammond, L. (2008). *Teaching for meaningful learning: A review of research on inquiry-based and cooperative learning.* In R. Furger's (Ed.), *Powerful learning: What we know about teaching for understanding,* (pp. 11–70). San Francisco, CA: Jossey-Bass.

Beatty, I. D., & Gerace, W. J. (2009). Technology-enhanced formative assessment: A research-based pedagogy for teaching science with classroom response technology. *Journal of Science Education and Technology, 18*(2), 146–162. doi:10.1007/s10956-008-9140-4

Biggs, J. B. (1993). From theory to practice: A cognitive systems approach. *Higher Education Research and Development, 12*(1), 73–85.

Black, P., Harrison, C., Lee, C., Marshall, B., & Wiliam, D. (2004). Working inside the black box: Assessment for learning in the classroom. *Phi Delta Kappan, 86*(1), 8–21.

Blumenfeld, P. C., Kempler, T. M., & Krajcik, J. S. (2006). Motivation and cognitive engagement in learning environments. In R. K. Sawyer (Ed.), *The Cambridge handbook of the learning sciences* (pp. 475–488). New York, NY: Cambridge University Press.

Bouillion, L. M., & Gomez, L. M. (2001). Connecting school and community with science learning: Real-world problems and school–community partnerships as contextual scaffolds. *Journal of Research in Science Teaching, 38*(8), 878–898.

Brady, J. (2014, Sept. 5). STEM is incredibly valuable, but if we want the best innovators we must teach the arts. *The Washington Post*, 5.

Burnaford, G., Brown, S., Doherty, J., & McLaughlin, H. J. (2007). Arts Integration Frameworks, Research Practice. Washington, DC: Arts Education Partnership.

Bybee, R. W. (2010). Advancing STEM education: A 2020 vision. *Technology and Engineering Teacher*, 70(1), 30.

Carnevale, A. P., Smith, N., & Melton, M. (2011). STEM: Science Technology Engineering Mathematics. Georgetown University Center on Education and the Workforce. Washington, D.C.

Clarke, J., & Dede, C. (2009). Design for scalability: A case study of the River City curriculum. *Journal of Science Education and Technology, 18*(4), 353–365.

Cohen, E. G., Lotan, R. A., Scarloss, B. A., & Arellano, A. R. (1999). Complex instruction: Equity in cooperative learning classrooms. *Theory into Practice, 38*(2), 80–86.

Collins, A., & Halverson, R. (2009). *Rethinking education in the age of technology: The digital revolution and schooling in America*. New York, NY: Teachers College Press.

Connor, A. M., Karmokar, S., & Whittington, C. (2015). From STEM to STEAM: Strategies for enhancing engineering & technology education. *International Journal of Engineering Pedagogy, 5*(2), 37–47.

Dede, C., & Richards, J. (Eds.). (2012). *Digital teaching platforms: Customizing classroom learning for each student*. New York, NY: Teachers College Press.

Delaney, M. (2014, April 2). Schools shift from STEM to STEAM. *EdTech*, 1–4. Retrieved from http://www.edtechmagazine.com/k12/article/2014/04/schools-shift-stem-steam

Educational Testing Service (ETS). (2015). *The STEM pipeline booklet*. Washington, DC: Inside Higher Ed. Retrieved from https://www.insidehighered.com/booklets

Galliot, A., Greens, R., Seddon, P., Wilson, M., & Woodham, J. (2011). Bridging STEM to STEAM: Trans-disciplinary research. *Centre for Research & Development, Research News, 28*, 20–23. Retrieved from http://arts.brighton.ac.uk/__data/assets/pdf_file/0006/43989/Research-News-28-on-line.pdf

Gayles, J. G. (Ed.). (2011). *Attracting and retaining women in STEM: New directions for institutional research, number 152* (Vol. 124). Tallahassee, FL: John Wiley & Sons.

Gibbs, P. (2015). Transdisciplinarity as epistemology, ontology or principles of practical judgment. In P. Gibbs (Ed.), *Transdisciplinary professional learning and practice* (pp. 151–164). London: Springer International Publishing.

Grimes, S. M., & Fields, D. A. (2012). *Kids online: A new research agenda for understanding social networking forums*. Retrieved from The Joan Ganz Cooney Center at Sesame Workshop website: http://www.joanganzcooneycenter.org/reports-38.html

Gulikers, J. T., Bastiaens, T. J., & Kirschner, P. A. (2004). A five-dimensional framework for authentic assessment. *Educational Technology Research and Development, 52*(3), 67.

Guyotte, K. W., Sochacka, N. W., Costantino, T. E., Walther, J., & Kellam, N. N. (2015). STEAM as social practice: Cultivating creativity in transdisciplinary spaces. *Art Education, 67*(6), 12–19.

Haney, J. J., Lumpe, A. T., & Czerniak, C. M. (2003). Constructivist beliefs about the science classroom learning environment: Perspectives from teachers, administrators, parents, community members, and students. *School Science and Mathematics, 103*(8), 366–377.

Harwell, M., Guzey, S. S., & Moore, T. J. (2016). Building up STEM: An analysis of teacher-developed engineering design-based STEM integration curricular materials. *Journal of Pre-College Engineering Education Research (J-PEER), 6*(1). doi:10.7771/2157-9288.1129

Haury, D. L. (1993). Teaching science through inquiry. *ERIC/CSMEE Digest* (ED 359 048). ERIC Clearinghouse for Science, Mathematics, and Environmental Education, Columbus, OH.

Henriksen, D. (2014). Full STEAM ahead: Creativity in excellent STEM teaching practices. *The STEAM Journal, 1*(2), 15.

Herro, D., & Quigley, C. (2016). Exploring teachers' perspectives of STEAM teaching: Implications for practice. *Journal of Professional Development in Education (PDE), 43*(3), 416–438. doi:10.1080/19415257.2016.1205507

Herro, D., Quigley, C., & Cian, H. (2018). The challenges of STEAM instruction: Lessons from the field. *Action in Teacher Education.* DOI: https://doi.org/10.1080/01626620.2018.1551159

Hill, C., Corbett, C., & St. Rose, A. (2010). *Why so few? Women in science, technology, engineering, and mathematics.* Washington, DC: American Association of University Women.

Ito, M., Gutiérrez, K., Livingstone S., Penuel, B., Rhodes, J., Salen, K., Schor, J., Sefton-Green, J., & Watkins, S. C. (2013). *Connected learning: An agenda for research and design.* Report for MacArthur Foundation Digital Media and Learning Research Hub. Retrieved from https://dmlhub.net/wp-content/uploads/files/Connected_Learning_report.pdf

Jaschick, S. (2014). Study finds increased STEM enrollment since the recession. *Inside Higher Ed*, 1–2.

Jenkins, H. (2008, June). Confessions of an Aca-daca fan. The official weblog of Henry Jenkins. [weblog]. Available at http://henryjenkins.org/2008/06/interview_with_total_recuts_ow.html

Jenkins, H., Clinton, K., Purushotma, R., Robison, A., & Weigel, M. (2006). *Confronting the challenges of participatory culture: Media education for the 21st century.* Chicago, IL: The MacArthur Foundation.

Johnson, L., Adams-Becker, S., Estrada, V., & Freeman, A. (2015). *NMC Horizon Report: Higher Education Edition.* Austin, Texas: The New Media Consortium.

Jolly, A. (2014). STEM vs. STEAM: Do the arts belong. *Education Week, 18.* Retrieved from http://www.edweek.org/tm/articles/2014/11/18/ctq-jolly-stem-vs-steam.html

Kilanowski-Press, L., Foote, C. J., & Rinaldo, V. J. (2010). Inclusion classrooms and teachers: A survey of current practices. *International Journal of Special Education, 25*(3), 43–56.

Kim, B. H., & Kim, J. (2016). Development and validation of evaluation indicators for teaching competency in STEAM education in Korea. *Eurasia Journal of Mathematics, Science & Technology Education, 12*(7), 1909–1924.

Kim, S. W., & Lee, Y. (2016). The analysis on research trends in programming-based STEAM education in Korea. *Indian Journal of Science and Technology, 9*(24), 1–11.

Kim, Y., & Park, N. (2012). Development and application of STEAM teaching model based on the Rube Goldberg's invention. In S. Yeo, Y. Pan, Y. Sun Lee, & H. Chang (Eds.), *Computer science and its applications* (pp. 693–698). Heidelberg, The Netherlands: Springer.

Krajcik, J., Blumenfeld, P. C., Marx, R. W., Bass, K. M., Fredricks, J., & Soloway, E. (1998). Inquiry in project-based science classrooms: Initial attempts by middle school students. *Journal of the Learning Sciences, 7*(3–4), 313–350.

Kruse, S., Louis, K. S., & Bryk, A. (1994). Building professional community in schools. *Issues in Restructuring Schools, 6*(3), 67–71.

Laboy-Rush, D. (2011). *Whitepaper: Integrated STEM education through project-based learning.* Retrieved from https://www.rondout.k12.ny.us/common/pages/DisplayFile.aspx?itemId=16466975

Lave, J. (1988). *Cognition in practice: Mind, mathematics and culture in everyday life.* Cambridge, UK: Cambridge University Press.

Lave, J., & Wenger, E. (1991). *Situated learning: Legitimate peripheral participation* (Vol. 29). Cambridge, UK: Cambridge University Press.

Lee, J., & Cramond, B. (1999). The positive effects of mentoring economically disadvantaged students. *Professional School Counseling, 2*(3), 172–178.

Liao, C. (2016). From interdisciplinary to transdisciplinary: An arts-integrated approach to STEAM education. *Art Education, 69*(6), 44–49.

Mallon, W. T., & Bunton, S. A. (2005). The functions of centers and institutes in academic biomedical research. *Analysis in Brief, 5*(1), 1–2.

Marks, H. M., & Printy, S. M. (2003). Principal leadership and school performance: An integration of transformational and instructional leadership. *Educational Administration Quarterly, 39*(3), 370–397. doi:10.1177/0013161X03253412

Masata, D. (2014). Understanding the STEM skills gap. *STEM Education News.* Retrieved from http://www.educationandcareernews.com

McTighe, J., & Wiggins, G. (2013). *Essential questions: Opening doors to student understanding.* Alexandria, VA: Association for Supervision and Curriculum Development (ASCD).

Miller, A. (2015) How to write driving questions. *Edutopia.* Retrieved from https://www.edutopia.org/blog/pbl-how-to-write-driving-questions-andrew-miller

Moriwaki, K., Brucker-Cohen, J., Campbell, L., Saavedra, J., Stark, L., & Taylor, L. (2012, March). Scrapyard Challenge Jr., adapting an art and design workshop to support STEM to STEAM learning experiences. In *Integrated STEM*

Education Conference (ISEC), 2nd Edition (pp. 1–6). Institude of Electrical and Electronics Engineers (IEEE).

Morris, E. W. (2007). "Ladies" or "loudies"? Perceptions and experiences of black girls in classrooms. *Youth and Society, 38*(4), 490–515.

Morrison, J. (2006). TIES STEM education monograph series, attributes of STEM education. Teaching Institute for Essential Science, Suffolk, VA.

Pescarmona, I. (2014). Learning to participate through complex instruction. *Intercultural Education, 25*(3), 187–196.

Peppler, K., & Bender, S. (2013). Maker movement spreads innovation one project at a time. *Phi Delta Kappan, 95*(3), 22–27.

Pohl, C. (2005). Transdisciplinary collaboration in environmental research. *Futures, 37*(10), 1159–1178.

Portz, S. (2015). The challenges of STEM education, paper 3. *Proceedings of the 43rd Space Congress: A Showcase of Space, Aviation, Technology, Logistics and Manufacturing*, Daytona Beach, Florida. Retrieved from Embry-Riddle Aeronautical University-Digital Commons,, http://commons.erau.edu/space-congress-proceedings/proceedings-2015-43rd/

Quigley, C. F., & Herro, D. (2016). "Finding the joy in the unknown": Implementation of STEAM teaching practices in middle school science and math classrooms. *Journal of Science Education and Technology, 25*(3), 410–426.

Quigley, C. F., Herro, D., & Jamil, F. M. (2017). Developing a conceptual model of STEAM teaching practices. *School Science and Mathematics, 117*(1–2), 1–12.

Radziwill, N. M., Benton, M. C., & Moellers, C. (2015). From STEM to STEAM: Reframing what it means to learn. *The STEAM Journal, 2*(1), 3.

Rittel, H. W. J., & Webber, M. M. (1974). Wicked problems. *Man-made Futures, 26*(1), 272–280.

Schummer, J. (2004). Interdisciplinary issues in nanoscale research. In D. Baird, A. Nordmann, & J. Schummer (Eds.), *Discovering the nanoscale* (pp. 9–20). Amsterdam, The Netherlands: IOS Press.

Shaffer, D. W. (2006). *How computer games help children learn.* New York, NY: Palgrave/Macmillan.

Silverstein, L. B., & Layne, S. (2010). *Defining arts integration* [PDF document]. Retrieved from The John F. Kennedy Center for the Performing Arts website: http://www.kennedy-center.org/education/partners/Defining_Arts_Integration.pdf

Skoretz, Y., & Childress, R. (2013). An evaluation of a school-based, job-embedded professional development program on teachers' efficacy for technology integration: Findings from an initial study. *Journal of Technology and Teacher Education, 21*(4), 461–484.

Smilan, C., & Miraglia, K. M. (2009). Art teachers as leaders of authentic art integration. *Art Education, 62*(6), 39–45.

Son, Y., Jung, S., Kwon, S., Kim, H., & Kim, D. (2012). Analysis of prospective and in-service teachers' awareness of steam convergent education. *Journal of Humanities & Social Science, 13*(1), 255–284.

Sousa, D. A., & Pilecki, T. (2013). *From STEM to STEAM: Using brain-compatible strategies to integrate the arts*. Thousand Oaks, CA: Corwin Press.

South Carolina Department of Education (2011). *South Carolina Social Studies Academic Standards*. Columbia, SC: Author.

Stefanou, C. R., Perencevich, K. C., DiCintio, M., & Turner, J. C. (2004). Supporting autonomy in the classroom: Ways teachers encourage student decision making and ownership. *Educational Psychologist, 39*(2), 97–110.

Stevens, R., Jona, K., Penney, L., Champion, D., Ramey, K. E., Hilppö, J., . . . & Penuel, W. (2016). *FUSE: An alternative infrastructure for empowering learners in schools*. Paper presented at International ConCLS Conference, held June 20–24, Singapore: International Society of the Learning Sciences.

Tomlinson, C. A. (2000). Reconcilable differences: Standards-based teaching and differentiation. *Educational Leadership, 58*(1), 6–13.

Tsurusaki, B. K., Tzou, C., Conner, L. D. C., & Guthrie, M. (2017). 5th–7th grade girls' conceptions of creativity: Implications for STEAM education. *Creative Education, 8*(2), 255–271. doi:10.4236/ce.2017.82020

U.S. Census Bureau. (2010). *American community survey. Selected characteristics of the native and foreign-born populations: 2011 American Community Survey 1-year estimates*. Washington, DC: Author.

Walsh, M. E., & Backe, S. (2013). School–university partnerships: Reflections and opportunities. *Peabody Journal of Education, 88(5)*, 594–607.

Wang, H. H., Moore, T. J., Roehrig, G. H., & Park, M. S. (2011). STEM integration: Teacher perceptions and practice. *Journal of Pre-College Engineering Education Research, 1*(2), 1–13.

What Is Connected Learning? (n.d.). Connected Learning Alliance. Retrieved from https://clalliance.org/why-connected-learning/

Williams, J. (2011). STEM education: Proceed with caution. *Design and Technology Education: An International Journal, 16*(1), 26–35.

Williams, L. (2013). Should STEM become STEAM? *District Administration, 49*(2), 22.

Wiggins, G. P., & McTighe, J. (2005). *Understanding by design*. Alexandria, VA: Association for Supervision and Curriculum Development (ASCD).

Wynn, T., & Harris, J. (2012). Toward a STEM+ arts curriculum: Creating the teacher team. *Art Education, 65*(5), 42–47.

Index

About the Authors

Cassie Quigley is an associate professor of science education in the Department of Instruction and Learning at the School of Education at the University of Pittsburgh. She received her doctorate in Curriculum and Instruction at Indiana University. Previously, as a middle and high school science teacher, Dr. Quigley witnessed how engaged students became when solving real-world problems in her classroom. This work led her to pursue a doctorate to understand specific instructional practices that would ensure that all students were engaged in science classrooms. Her research focuses on broadening the conceptions of and participation in science, which is how she became turned on to STEAM teaching. She sees STEAM as a way to connect students to science through a transdisciplinary, problem-solving approach. She works with inservice and preservice teachers on expanding their current pedagogical practices to include STEAM approaches. Dr. Quigley also teaches preservice science teachers as well as graduate students at the University of Pittsburgh.

Danielle Herro is an associate professor of digital media and learning at Clemson University in the Learning Sciences department. She received her doctorate in Curriculum and Instruction at the University of Wisconsin–Madison. Dr. Herro teaches courses on social media, games, and emerging technologies, and she co-designed and opened the Digital Media and Learning and Gaming Labs in Clemson's College of Education. She has published numerous journal articles on the impact of bringing game-based, mobile, and other digital media environments to K–12 schools. Her current research focuses on investigating the intersection of games, identity, and social practices, and the efficacy of teacher professional development toward integrating STEAM education. She has worked extensively with administrators and teachers to realize STEAM education initiatives in K–12 classrooms, assisting administrators with conceptualizing STEAM education and teachers with creating STEAM instructional units. She hopes to provide guidance and best practices for all educators wishing to embrace STEAM education as an interest-based, engaging way to facilitate equitable participation for their students in problem solving across disciplines.